This is a book about one of life's greatest pleasures: getting something for nothing. If you have the nerve, there *is* such a thing as a free lunch. The author brings to the subject over forty years of experience as a freeloader, bearing always in mind the example of his father: 'He managed to suggest that making enough money with which to *buy* whatever one wanted was at best rather caddish, if not actually downright immoral'.

With illustrations by Nicholas Garland, this witty, instructive and amusing book is the perfect gift for all freeloaders, whether practising or armchair.

THE JOY OF
FREELOADING

PATRICK SKENE CATLING

With illustrations by Nicholas Garland

HOW TO HAVE A TERRIFIC TIME
AT SOMEONE ELSE'S EXPENSE

BLOOMSBURY

First published in Great Britain 1990

Copyright © Patrick Skene Catling 1990

Illustrations copyright © Nicholas Garland 1990

The moral right of the author has been asserted

Bloomsbury Publishing Ltd, 2 Soho Square, London W1V 5DE

A CIP catalogue record for this book is
available from the British Library

ISBN 0 7475 0702 3

10 9 8 7 6 5 4 3 2 1

Photoset by Rowland Phototypesetting Ltd,
Bury St Edmunds, Suffolk
Printed and bound in Great Britain by
Richard Clay Ltd, Bungay, Suffolk

'In my youth,' father William replied to his son,
'I feared it might injure the brain;
But now that I'm perfectly sure I have none,
Why, I do it again and again.'

Lewis Carroll

for
IRIS DIANA
and my brothers,
TIMOTHY & DUNCAN

ACKNOWLEDGEMENTS

The Prologue consists mainly of material originally published in *The Spectator*, whose permission to use it here is acknowledged with thanks.

Lines from *The Odes of Horace*, translated by James Michie, were published by Rupert Hart-Davis (1964).

The Pimm's Book of Polo by John Lloyd was published by Stanley Paul (1989).

Introduction

WHEN Patrick Skene Catling asked me to give him a push to get him started on this exemplary guide to freeloading, I was glad to do so. Dr Alex Comfort's *The Joy of Sex* was an amusing handbook; but Catling's *The Joy of Freeloading* penetrates to a deeper level of more reliable gratification. We discussed the matter at some length over dinner at the Savoy, which he was able somehow to arrange with his publisher. I hardly need mention that the wines were very interesting.

I have known Catling since school, where he used to exert himself with energy and ingenuity literally for peanuts. Since those early days, I have watched his career close up and at a distance, usually with approval and sometimes even with envy. As his senior, I can say, I hope without immodesty, that initially I put him on the right track, and from time to time I have given him the benefit of my own experience. It is a pleasure to vouch for him now as a journeyman freeloader.

The freeloader never openly applies the term to himself, of course, although in his heart he is proud to acknowledge himself as such. Most dictionaries pejoratively define a freeloader as a sponger or scrounger. Lexicographers are not noted for the tolerance of their value judgments; they often fail to keep in touch with contemporary reality. A true freeloader is a philanthropist in the purest sense, a lover of humankind. He operates with careful decorum, and never stings the needy.

Freeloading is a philosophy, a way of life, and a challenge. Sitting here in the snug study of my grace-and-favour apartment in St James's Palace, I recognise that the freeloader is something of a visionary. He sees the need to correct the imbalances of the consumer economy, by taking out of it more than he puts in, by getting a lot for a little, by having a feast without a reckoning. Improving on the Bible, he believes that to him that hath not it

2

should be given. Is it too much to call him a modern hero, a latterday Robin Hood? The freeloader takes from the rich and gives to himself.

The freeloader must comprehend materialism, if he is to rise above it. He must be aware of the basic pecuniary necessities, those 'upfront' investments known in show business as 'seed money', 'walking-around money' and 'eating money'. But the freeloader should not allow himself to become a mercenary vulgarian. He should practise freeloading as an art form, largely for its own sake. When the flow of one's disposable income is in full spate, one may be pleased to dispose of some of it, within reason; however, dispensing personal funds cannot offer anything comparable with the excitement and satisfaction of analysing and solving a problem in freeloading, like a problem in differential calculus or croquet.

Catling does not actually state his credo, except, perhaps, obliquely, by implication. But his actions (and inactions) clearly demonstrate that he adheres meticulously to the ethical and technical principles of freeloading. He understands that it is unethical (and usually unnecessary) to lie to potential benefactors, yet it is acceptable to allow them to jump to useful conclusions. The freeloader must know how to appeal to generosity, vanity and greed, and when it is all right to wear stripes with paisley. At its most advanced, freeloading is a commitment.

As my late kinsman, J. B. Overly, the distinguished deficit financier, put it so well: 'Total credit is not for the faint of heart; but for total consumers nothing less will do.' He was a child prodigy. He was only four when he first persuaded a Highgate confectioner to give him four ounces of liquorice allsorts on tick. In his later years, he kept his first tailor's bill, framed, on the wall of the library of his National Trust castle.

'The neophyte credit-purchaser must establish an initial portfolio of charge accounts *all at once*,' he used to say, 'and attack them boldly *all at once*. There is nothing that gives a creditor a sense of anxiety more precipitously than loneliness. Credit must be used, and it must be seen to be used.'

With all due respect to J. B.'s memory, I must say that there was a certain brashness about his methods. We have come a long way since his time. Freeloading is quite a different sort of procedure, necessarily subtle and usually unnoticeable, except sometimes in retrospect.

I can easily understand why Catling wishes to reveal some of his successful freeloading endeavours. No artist is content for ever to create in a void; he craves appreciative feedback. I, myself, have often wanted to share my reminiscences of loads freely gained. I was delighted when Catling recently asked my permission to tell the world about our elegant airport scam (see the Prologue). Unfortunately, whenever any freeloading scenario becomes generally known there is an immediate danger of obsolescence. But I feel sure that this book will inspire many would-be freeloaders to devise imaginative and daring original schemes of their own. One of the beauties of freeloading is its infinite open-endedness. Though Catling is occasionally surprisingly candid in the following pages, I am confident that he has withheld a few secrets for future use.

Vincent Overly

Prologue

I'D like to begin with a tribute to my old mentor. Vincent Overly, after several decades of freeloading, is still one of the great innovators. In chess terms, he is a grand master. There are times when he has to be, in order to maintain his high standard of living. His mysterious operations in the City of London have had some dramatic ups and downs, but a graph of his private way of life would be a simple, smooth vector of continuous, gradual ascendancy.

About a year ago, having, in his words, 'stubbed one's toe in the City, rather painfully, actually,' he was resting longer than usual. He complained that he was 'frightfully broke'. This was shortly before he moved into St James's Palace ('Her Majesty is jolly nice'), which he finds handy for backgammon at Boodle's.

'During the present hiatus,' he told me on the telephone one morning, 'it is important to maintain one's morale, keep the wits well honed, and so on. Are you doing anything for lunch?'

As it happened, I was not busy. In memory of his lavish hospitality in the past (he had alerted me to the opening of many a new restaurant), I was glad to be able to treat him to a meal.

'The Connaught?' I suggested, not without a certain apprehensiveness, for he has a penchant for rare game birds, and I have never been as rich as he sometimes is.

'No, no, no!' he protested genially. 'I'm not asking you to ask me to lunch. This expedition was my idea. All I want from you is your company. Almost all.'

'But surely it's my turn,' I murmured.

'No. This little outing is something I thought up just today in the bath. It'll do both of us a lot of good. It may well change the pattern of social life as we know it. In addition to your presence, actually there is one contribution I need from you.'

6

Oh, I thought. Here it comes.

'Are you still there?' he asked.

'Yes,' I admitted.

'You have to bring some cash.'

'Yes,' I said with a sigh. Of course. 'How much?'

'Enough for two tickets from London to Paris.'

'Paris!' That must mean the Tour d'Argent or the Grand Véfour or at least the Crillon. Wasn't that rather extravagant, even for someone whose morale needed a boost?

'Paris,' he confirmed. 'First class.'

'London – Paris first-class return must be – ' I could only hazard a guess. I fly to Paris only infrequently, and then always executive class, or even economy.

'First class,' he repeated emphatically. 'But not return. I've checked on the one-way fare.' This was in the peak season. 'It's £167 – £334 for the two of us.' Some lunch! And that was what it would cost the *guest*.

'But Vincent – '

'Why only one way?' he said, as if reading my mind. Even over the telephone, I could detect his characteristically cryptic smile. He enjoys mystifying others. 'That's all you have to bring,' he assured me. 'In cash, please. You'll see soon enough how it's all going to work out. You'll get your money back.'

How and when, I wondered, not very optimistically. I trust him but there are times when he seems *mañana*-oriented. Was he counting on funds from some French business associate? As far as I knew, he had dealings with only a charming but languid marquis, whose principal function was to add Continental *éclat* to Vincent's letterhead.

Having pocketed my passport, the British one, and visited my preferred bank, I took a taxi to Vincent's mews house in Belgravia. He was already outside the yellow door, dressed in a cheerful tweed suit, a soft brown hat and brown suede shoes, as if going to an informal race meeting. He was wearing a red carnation in his buttonhole and a grin on his roundish, pink face, so I realised he was in a playful mood, though there was evidently no time for us to have a stirrup cup. I wished I were in a playful mood.

Slamming the taxi door behind him, he told the driver to take us to Heathrow.

'Which terminal, guv?'

Vincent said he wanted the one from which planes left for Paris, and told him the name of the airline.

'Why that one?' I asked. I wasn't objecting; I was merely curious. It was a long-established, reputable national airline, but not the one that would first have sprung to mind.

'Their new advertising campaign is incomparably superior to the others,' Vincent replied. 'They are really trying to please. Haven't you noticed? They obviously understand about food and drink. They sympathise with gluttons. Their stewardesses are the prettiest.'

At the airport, I gave Vincent the money. He went to get the tickets, while I looked at magazines.

'What's our flight?' I asked. I like to be on time. He smiled complacently.

'The 4.50,' he said.

'4.50! I thought we were going to have lunch.'

'We are. Oh, we are!'

He led the way to the newly redecorated first-class departure lounge, whose luxurious facilities are open, of course, only to bearers of first-class tickets. Vincent uttered a conventional pleasantry or two as he showed our tickets, and the beautiful hostess beamed as warmly as a breakfast-show presenter.

The lounge was gently animated by the small talk of elegant men and women. The place was not crowded. Everything about it was pleasantly soft: the music was soft; softly upholstered, dull-golden armchairs were disposed here and there in discreetly separated groups; the dark saffron carpet was soft on the way to the long, richly-stocked bar and buffet.

'Champagne first, don't you agree?' Vincent suggested. 'I always say it's the best thing to rinse the taste buds with, early in the day.' A softly illuminated golden clock on the wall indicated that the time was 11.40, five hours and ten minutes to our scheduled time of takeoff. Champagne, I thought, was a good idea.

'Have you any Bollinger?' Vincent enquired of the young blonde barmaid, whose voluptuousness mocked the restriction of her well-cut uniform. 'Or Veuve Clicquot would do.' Thus began the first of many interesting discussions which enlivened the hours.

'The champagne is Piper-Heidsieck,' the barmaid informed us. 'Is that all right?'

'Quite all right,' Vincent assured her encouragingly. 'I like its fullness and dryness and all-round friendly demeanour. Let us, by all means, have some of that.'

We found that we were thirsty. The first bottle went fast. As we thoughtfully sipped a second, Vincent moved, and I followed, in a leisurely fashion along the bar to inspect the buffet counter. We found a tempting array of hors d'oeuvres, smoked salmon and trout, shrimps and lobster, cold turkey, ham and rare roast beef, salads, fresh fruit and an assortment of classic cheeses.

'It all looks eminently satisfactory,' he commented approvingly, spearing an anchovy-stuffed olive with a pointed swizzle stick. 'There's absolutely no rush, mind you, but it's nice to know it's all here. For the moment, perhaps just some of this pâté.' He tasted it. 'Mmm! Smoked mackerel. Delicious. At this point, I do believe I'll switch to Chablis.'

After we had passed some time sampling various excellent white Burgundies, we took a series of carefully laden dishes to a convenient table for two.

'I wonder how they keep track of all we're having,' I said – naïvely, I know now. Vincent has the invaluable knack of suspending other people's disbelief. For the moment, I was as credulous as a beginner.

' "Keep track"?' he echoed with a frown of aesthetic distress. 'Why would they wish to do that? There's no time limit here for passengers awaiting their flights. There's no limit to what they may eat and drink. And, of course, there is no charge.'

These considerations greatly stimulated my appetite. When sated with seafood, I helped myself to a generous selection of cold meats. The beef was perfectly moist and tender. Vincent, also having progressed to the more serious viands, soon announced his approval of the claret.

'This,' he solemnly averred, 'is a quite exceptionally jolly Pauillac. Call me sentimental if you will, but Lynch-Bages has always been a favourite of mine.'

The afternoon gradually latened and we noticeably mellowed, and I suddenly became concerned about the time. It was 4.05.

'Yes,' Vincent acknowledged, 'it is almost time to go. I'll have only one more port with this splendid Stilton. We can leave the Armagnac for another time.'

He paused at the reception desk to give the hostess our compliments, some of which were to be conveyed to the chef and the sommelier, our congratulations to the airline and our warmest thanks.

'I don't see how we'll be able to appreciate Paris after all that,' I said. Vincent smiled, a bit sleepily.

'Nor do I,' he said.

Then, to my surprise, he led the way back to the ticket counter. They honoured without question our request for cancellation and immediately gave us a full refund.

'Here you are,' Vincent said smugly. 'Your £334, as good as new.'

I gratefully stuffed the money into a pocket, and didn't mind when he stuck me again for the taxi. One keeps learning.

LORD WEIDENFELD, the publisher, received me in his flat on the Chelsea Embankment when he was Sir George. He had been plain George at the time of our first meeting, not very many years after his ambitious migration from Vienna. Then we were both gratefully eating couscous, the simple North African wheaten dish, and drinking Algerian red plonk in a less fashionable part of Chelsea, in Lady Jane Heaton's basement kitchen. Even back in those days, he had a thing about titles. He eventually got the one he wanted from Harold Wilson, who was demanding but not fastidious. Now George was reclining at ease in a deep armchair in his splendid library, and I was balancing on the edge of a shallow chair at his feet. I was wondering whether *noblesse* would *oblige*.

The smooth complexion of his plump cheeks gave an impression of hot towels, creamy lotions and massage. His lapels were conspicuously hand-stitched, the widely separated stitches giving the edges of the lapels that slightly crinkled, Roman-tailored look. His neat, gleaming fingernails adorned the great brown cylinder of his corona corona. I perceived cologne.

After a solicitous consultation, he ordered the butler to bring me a Tio Pepe. In a delicate glass on a Georgian silver tray, the sherry was wafted to my side.

I told George about my new scheme for programming dreams by implanting electrodes into the brain. He gazed at me with heavy-lidded, large, moist, dark, contented eyes and smiled tolerantly.

'An amusing idea,' he said. 'But I'm sorry to have to say that there is a slight, temporary impediment in the cash flow.'

All I had said I wanted was some cash for a novel I had not yet begun to write. Was that asking too much? I looked around with raised eyebrows at the sumptuously carpeted room (at that very moment, the butler was silently approaching us again), at the shelves of leatherbound books, the Flemish tapestries, the large Francis Bacon painting above the fireplace. George recognised my expression as one of incredulity and added:

'Oh, no, Patrick, not mine – yours.'

How we laughed! Especially George.

He stood and I stood.

'Perhaps I'll be able to work something out,' he said. 'In the meantime, where are you heading? My man can drive you. So much easier than finding a taxi here at this hour.'

'The Dorchester,' I replied, not wishing to say where I was really staying.

In the quiet, fragrant comfort of George's car, I counted the evening's gains. They were shelter from the rain, two sherries, a free ride, and a valuable lesson: never try to hustle an expert.

I was a beginner.

AS Hazlitt correctly pointed out, 'It is hard to be without money. To get on without it is like travelling in a foreign country without a passport – you are stopped, suspected, and made ridiculous at every turn, besides being subjected to the most serious inconveniences.'

By and large, conditions have improved since Hazlitt's time (1778–1830). Relief is to be found in many places. Among them, first-class hotels can prove to be especially helpful.

Quite a long time ago, I bought an attaché case in a London railway lost-property shop. It was not the kind of case now advertised in *Harpers & Queen* and the *New Yorker*. Evidently it had been constructed hastily with ill-fitting sheets of lacquered cardboard. But then I went to one of those shops which help to give Shaftesbury Avenue its special ambience, where they sell gilded models of Big Ben, whoopee cushions, and packets of assorted hotel labels. Once I had decorated the case with the labels of Raffles, Mena House, the Imperial Hotel in Tokyo and the Royal Victoria Hotel, Nassau, even though not all of them were still open for business, the case and I were treated with respect. It enabled me to face doormen, porters and reception-ists without blenching. And sustained by that confidence I no longer had to rely entirely on personal credentials.

Hotelkeepers are human. Once in Bombay I checked into the Taj Hotel, a splendid old institution retaining some of the more admirable features of the Raj. The building itself is impressively substantial and well situated close to the waterfront arch known as the Gateway of India. However, things being as they were at the time, I was able to afford only one of the smallest rooms available. My spirits sank as a turbaned porter led me down a long, narrow corridor to the backside of the hotel. At the far end of the corridor, a workman stripped to the waist was

16

convulsed by a pneumatic drill. It was pounding with the racket of a heavy machine gun, in a grey cloud of grit from the pulverised marble floor.

'– –, –,' said the porter, unlocking the last door. His voice was inaudible in the roar of the engine and the hammering of steel against marble.

'WHAT?' I shouted.

'YOUR ROOM, SAHIB,' he repeated, standing aside to let me in. The room was twice the width of the single bed. The only other furniture was a free-standing wardrobe and a small wooden chair at a table bearing a Victorian china washbowl, jug and soap dish. The window gave onto a blank wall.

I must have looked unhappy as I proffered a few rupees; with an embarrassed smile, he refused to accept the tip.

Without having the heart to unpack my suitcase, I immediately got out of that claustrophobic cell and set forth on the long trek back to the lift. In the lobby, handsome Indians in white linen suits were conversing in whispers with beautiful ladies in silken saris of many colours, magenta, emerald and peacock blue. There was a faint erotic scent of sandalwood and Rive Gauche. I felt as though my blood had been diluted with lukewarm water. And then, of course, as usually happens at times of dire emergency, an idea flashed like the traditional comic-strip light bulb.

At the reception desk, I requested an audience with the manager.

'The manager is engaged at present, sir,' the receptionist suavely informed me.

'I'll wait,' I said in a voice of calm determination.

'He's quite busy, sir. Perhaps I could be of some assistance?'

'No, thank you. This is a personal matter.'

He appraised me carefully and apparently saw that I was prepared to wait for ever, possibly spoiling his day.

The manager, dressed like a nineteenth-century British ambassador, all black and grey, was sitting behind a large mahogany desk in a large, formal office with a high ceiling and tall windows.

After the customary exchange of identities, he smiled and said: 'Everything is satisfactory, I trust.'

I smiled and shrugged acquiescently.

'That isn't why I wished to meet you,' I said. 'I only wanted to tell you how delighted I am to be here in your famous hotel, for the first time.'

'Oh,' he said, slightly off balance. 'We are pleased to provide accommodation.'

'My father and mother stayed here in 1925, on their honeymoon. They travelled from Bangalore specially to stay at the Taj. Their friends in Bombay arranged a second wedding reception at the hotel. It was magnificent! One of the happiest memories of their years in India. In my family, the Taj is a legend.'

The manager looked genuinely touched.

'That is very nice,' he said.

'That's all I wished to tell you.'

He stood and we shook hands.

'We're looking after you, of course?' he said.

'I've just arrived,' I told him.

'What is your room number?'

I glanced casually at my key. He accepted the information without betraying any emotion.

'Well,' I said, 'thank you for receiving me. I'm going to the dining room for some lunch.'

'We hope you will enjoy your stay,' he said.

I left my key at the desk and went and had an excellent lunch. The lamb was particularly good. And I'm fond of custard apples. Perhaps I was rather greedy. Anyway, when I found that the second cup of coffee was failing to keep me wide awake, I decided I would have a nap before getting ready for the evening.

The receptionist seemed deferential as he handed me my key. It was a different key. It was the key to the bridal suite.

A few days later, when I requested the cashier to prepare my bill, he graciously bowed his head, smiled charmingly, and said that there wasn't one.

In the taxi, I sincerely wished that my parents had spent their honeymoon in Bombay. They might have.

The 'family legend' ploy would probably get one nowhere in most occidental hotels, but it is worth remembering in long-established ones that cherish reputations for hospitality in the grand manner.

There are still a few splendid hotels in London. I was walking along Piccadilly early one fine Saturday, the sort of morning that might have moved Bertie Wooster to click his heels, allude to half-remembered lyrical fragments of Shakespeare and exclaim 'What-ho!' It was a few minutes after opening time, but I had a letter to post, explaining some petty transaction. I wanted the letter to reach my bank manager by Monday. He is a tolerant fellow but there are times when he feels he should abide by head-office rules. On reaching the arcade of the Ritz, I decided to pop in for a stamp. The day was ideal for popping in to places.

I entered through the main doors. The desk of the concierge is near the distant side door, so I was able to approach him from the interior of the hotel. Perhaps he would have greeted me with old-fashioned obsequiousness even if he had seen me come in from the street; anyway, I got an ego rub *de luxe* for only a few pence. He seemed really interested in my opinion of the weather. I felt as if I belonged there. Proceeding blithely along the foyer, I felt my spirits further uplifted when I encountered a hero.

It is important to remember, as Vincent has reminded me time and time again, that most celebrities quite like being recognised by strangers in public places. Only minor ones, often unrecognised, pretend that they prefer always to remain incognito. A bold approach is surprisingly often not unwelcome.

Graham Greene was in London, staying as usual at the Ritz, for the opening of a new production of one of his plays, *The Potting Shed*, I believe. Having just flown up from his home in Antibes, he was looking exceptionally fit. A Riviera tan looks much healthier than a gloomily lighted portrait by Karsh of Ottawa. I had never met Mr Greene before, but I knew the book-jacket photograph well. His face in full Ritzcolour was encouraging, so I accosted him. I used the West Cork opening.

'Mr Greene?'

He stopped, with a polite, interrogative half-smile.

'Yes?'

'I wonder whether there's any possibility of persuading you to have a drink?'

'Yes, certainly.'

'But not here,' I added. The Rivoli Bar did not seem right for a sunny morning. It was daring, perhaps even impertinent, to attach strings to my proposal; but the strings may have had a novelty appeal to the great man. He didn't turn a hair. (How, by the way, does one turn a hair?)

'I agree,' he said decisively. 'I know just the place.'

He turned and led the way out of the hotel.

Unspeaking, we walked down St James's Street at the brisk pace of men who are mindful that the pubs have already been open for nearly a quarter of an hour. Left on King Street and right down Crown Passage, we came to a well-hidden, small pub that I later recognised on the first page of *The Human Factor*. The pub seemed perfect for an MI6 agent resting between engagements.

The barman obviously knew Mr Greene of old. Without a word having been said, two pints of bitter were drawn and placed on the bar before us.

Still wordless, we drank a few long swallows of the cool, flat beer. Mr Greene put down his glass.

'This isn't doing much good, is it?' he said.

'No,' I agreed.

At that moment it became apparent that he was in charge. He had assumed the role of host and I was a guest. Some subliminal recognition may have reminded him of the days when he and his wife were living in a cottage in Chipping Camden, on the edge of the Cotswolds. The rent was only one pound a week but there were rats in the roof. He remembers Orwellian penury. He likes buying people drinks.

A subtle signal of his caused the barman to serve two large pink gins. They contained only a hint of Angostura and not much water. Then we started talking, and the pink gins continually arrived as though by magic.

Graham Greene once won a prize in a competition in a London weekly with a parody of Graham Greene. He is good at composing Graham Greene lines. One of his recent novels, *Monsignor Quixote*, in which a Spanish priest and a communist ex-mayor travel together, drink wine and dispute their beliefs, provides many fine examples.

When we found ourselves discussing publishers, he said of one of them: 'He's a thief and a fool – a dangerous combination.'

On the more controversial subject of God, Mr Greene said: 'Don't be too concerned about doubts. A faith without doubts seems to me inhuman. There must be doubts about a mystery.'

I think he eventually walked back to the Ritz. I don't remember where I went. It had been a richly productive stamp.

3

ROYAL warrants are conferred upon manufacturers only after rigorous tests have proved satisfactory. When I see the royal coat of arms on a label I drink with confidence and pride. If a bottle of vodka was distilled 'By Appointment' it is almost sure to be good stuff. After all, the royal family have been handing out warrants for the past one hundred and fifty years. They have standards to maintain. Are they pestered by salesmen offering free samples? I suppose so. The late Duke of Windsor was internationally renowned for freeloading, but only in exile. I never noticed him put his hand in his pocket at the bar after golf when he was the Governor of the Bahamas. To me, he was an inspiration; however, it is unlikely that the present sovereign would wish to compete with her uncle on that level.

At the breakfast table one summer morning, reading the Kellogg's Country Store Box ('By appointment to HM the Queen, Purveyors of Cereals'), which was more interesting, because newer, than the familiar marmalade jar, I said to myself, and I quote: 'I bet Her Majesty serves a lovely cup of tea.'

At Buckingham Palace every summer there are several teatime garden parties. There should be more of them. Think how many admirers of the monarchy never get to one. There are usually only about nine thousand guests at each party. Even if there were one a week (there isn't), it is doubtful that the supply of tickets would ever exceed the demand.

I once suggested to the Lord Chamberlain, by letter, that he, or whoever manages such things, should organise more frequent Palace tea parties, to gratify a larger number of loyal subjects and, even more importantly, to attract more of the right class of tourists from abroad. Foreigners registering at approved hotels, such as the Basil Street Hotel and the Stafford, should be awarded numbered chances in a weekly lottery for invitations to the

22

Palace. Perhaps the Queen would not wish to preside over every party in person; Elizabeth II lookalikes could be hired sometimes in her place. Very few guests are presented to her at the parties, and those who are must be too flustered to inspect her closely for genuineness. If there were any anxiety about possible detection of imposture, a few suitable fake guests could be recruited for the presentations. The only response to my letter, however, was a terse printed acknowledgement, without comment, so there may be no immediate intention to initiate my scheme.

How was I to wangle my way into that exclusive enclave for tea? Tea at Fortnum & Mason's was all very well in its way, but I was beginning to feel that it was too costly for what it was. Socially, it was insufficiently fulfilling.

Having studied authoritative reports of the Palace tea parties of previous seasons (Albany in the *Sunday Telegraph* and Jennifer in her monthly Diary often seem to know what they are writing about), I realised that to qualify easily for admission I should have been a fairly senior civil servant, a commissioned officer or an Anglican bishop from some not-too-violent Commonwealth country, or a United Kingdom bureaucrat, preferably well connected with the Women's Institute, the Chelsea Flower Show and the Westminster Kennel Club. But, I reasoned with whitening knuckles, there must be other ways. There are.

Fortunately for would-be self-invited guests, Palace security is lax. Who needs to be reminded of Michael Fagan, the young man who climbed through a Palace window and got into the Queen's bedroom when the Queen herself was in it?

I considered dressing in black leather and a helmet and arriving on a motorcycle at the Palace tradesmen's entrance some party afternoon. In London, nobody ever stops a motorcycle messenger; they are always in such a hurry and such a bad temper that it is almost impossible to speak to them: no door is barred. I was sure that once I got through the Buckingham Palace Road gateway to the Royal Mews I would have no difficulty in sneaking around to the back of the tea tent, where I would change into the proper costume carried in my parcel marked URGENT.

Another quite simple method of effecting entry into the hallowed garden, I thought, would be to ingratiate myself with a *bona fide* employee of J. Lyons & Co., the firm that does the catering. On the day, I would dress as a member of the staff of that respected organisation and change my clothes in a staff loo. But that way also would lack dignity, without which a royal tea is nothing. The whole caper would be a hollow mockery of the pageant of which I aspired to be a part.

I must admit that I was close to abandoning hope when I read in *The Times* about the forthcoming convention of the American Bar Association. One should always keep an eye on the quality press for this sort of news; it offers many opportunities. Several thousand American lawyers and their spouses were coming to London for their annual get-together, and they had been invited en masse to a garden party specially for them at the Palace.

London is crowded with visitors at all times of the year, but the highest season, of course, is midsummer. Millions of visitors throng there from all over the world. They are eager to find Madame Tussaud's and the Crown Jewels, photograph each other during the Changing of the Guard, and eat Big Macs. Many of the natives and other local inhabitants, tiring of interpreting the visitors' small-scale street maps and explaining the Underground railway system, irritably give false directions. This practice is not only boorish and unkind; it is a foolish self-deprivation of the golden benefits of international friendship. Even in the elbowing hurly-burly of Oxford Street and Piccadilly Circus, one should always be courteous and alert to potential benefits.

I knew that most American lawyers must be more sophisticated than the average farmer from Zaire and that they would have a sense of proportion about historic sightseeing and other means of recreation. Some of them, no doubt, would be looking for The Old Curiosity Shop; others, on the other hand, would probably be looking for authentic dry martinis, and have sound ideas about where to find them.

The American Bar at the Savoy was full of seersucker and madras jackets that summer. I had disguised myself for the occasion in Ivy-League summer uniform – a slightly crumpled olive-green cotton suit by Haspel, a button-down blue Sea Island cotton shirt by Albercrombie & Fitch, a pseudo-regimental red-and-blue striped silk tie by Countess Mara (a Christmas present), sand-coloured buckskin shoes with red rubber soles by Brooks Brothers, and a dull-green, dark blue and khaki Ancient Madder ornamental silk pocket handkerchief that I thought Tom Wolfe would have approved of. I believe that convincing facsimiles of the whole ensemble may now be purchased from any branch of Marks & Spencer's. I collected mine in the course of a Saturday-morning exploration of the used-clothing shops of Portobello Road.

As I gently forced my way to the bar, I could hear in the congenial babble the flat, long a's of New England speech, the attenuated aow's of the South and the interstate loud laughter of educated, high-income Americans in the middle of an away-from-home Happy Hour. Their motto was 'When in Rome, do as the New Yorkers do.' And why not? That's what Romans try to do.

'A Midleton Very Rare with a splash of Malvern water,' I instructed the barman.

'Sorry, sir,' he said with a frown that was both apologetic and puzzled, for he knew I usually asked for vodka and tonic. 'We're out of Midleton Very Rare at the moment.'

I would have been willing to bet that even the resourceful Savoy was unlikely to have any of the golden elixir. Midleton Very Rare is, indeed, very rare. It is advertised, very rarely, as 'Ireland's most exclusive whiskey'. Connoisseurs plead for it, often in vain. The only time I ever tasted it was in the Ball O'Malt Bar at the Irish Distillers' headquarters in Dublin, a bar I can unequivocally recommend. It is situated immediately adjacent to their museum, which is open to the public, by arrangement. After one passes through an exhibition of artefacts and pictures relating the history and showing the techniques of Irish whiskey distilling, one is welcomed to the bar to sample all the varieties of Ireland's national spirit. Whether travelling or staying close to home, I always bear in mind that distillers and brewers are the friendliest of hosts; a visit to their premises is generously rewarded, at no expense to the visitor.

I had requested Midleton Very Rare to draw attention to myself. I succeeded. Ordering an unusual drink is an effective method of opening a barroom conversation.

'We have Bushmill's Black Label,' the barman said.

'All right,' I allowed. 'A Black Bush with water.'

'Without ice, sir?'

'Of course.'

'Excuse me,' said the man by my side. If his nose had looked less intensively lived in, he might have resembled Paul Newman. Like one of those dear old boys in pink Leander caps at Henley, the man appeared to be a superannuated student. He was wearing an orange-and-black striped blazer, chinos and well-polished loafers. 'I couldn't help overhearing you. That Midleton Very Rare – is it a Scotch?'

'No. Irish.'

'Irish! Is that right? So, I assume then, is Black Bush.'

'Yes. Bushmill's is the oldest distillery in the world.'

'Is that so? That's very interesting. Good stuff, eh?'

'Scotch whisky is distilled twice. Irish whiskey is triple-distilled. Eliminates the poisonous fusel-oil. Smoother. Easier on the liver.'

'Hey, I think I'll try some of that.'

I ordered him a Black Bush.

'But let me get these,' he said, producing a fifty-pound note. He grinned. 'Monopoly money. The whole trip's deductible.'

I raised my glass in tribute to someone freeloading on the United States Government.

'Here's to tax deductions,' I said.

'I'll drink to that,' he responded. He took a thoughtful sip. 'This is nifty. It tastes like more.'

We had more.

'Are you here with the ABA?' he wondered.

'I haven't been a member of the Association for years,' I said with a regretful sigh, speaking the truth.

'That's too bad. We have a great convention program.'

'So I understand.'

'Are you an attorney now?'

'Not a practising one.' Also true, please note.

'What are you doing these days?'

I glanced over my shoulder, then looked back at him, candidly straight into the eyes. I leaned closer, tapped the side of my nose with a conspiratorial finger and whispered: 'This and that. If you know what I mean.'

He half-closed his eyes, protruded his lower lip and slowly nodded. The expression was one of inviolable professional confidentiality. I saw that he was becoming less sober.

'Are you an American or what?' he asked. 'You dress American.'

'I've lived over here for quite a while,' I said. With experience, one is able to answer such questions satisfactorily, without submitting to any invasion of privacy. However, I gave him my name, my only contribution to the proceedings.

'Hi,' he said, extending a friendly right hand. 'Chesley Brewster. C. Pinkney Brewster the Third. Princeton '53.'

I excused myself, made a telephone call, and returned.

'Chesley?' I said. 'May I call you Chesley?'

'Sure, Pat.'

'Chesley, how about a change of venue? There's a club I'd like to introduce you to.'

Major Warwick Charlton and the late Dick Brennan invented the Wig & Pen Club, opposite the Law Courts, at the Fleet Street end of the Strand. The wig represents the law and the pen represents the press. Fleet Street, it may be remembered, was once a street of newspaper offices. As in the case of many other London clubs nowadays, the Wig & Pen's membership base has been extensively broadened, for financial reasons. In fact, it has always been quite broad, admitting many men and women whose only interest in the law is that of any cautious citizen, and other members, called creative people, who deal with newspapers only from the outside, people in advertising, publicity and public relations, promoters and salesmen with fringe interests in the media.

Warwick is an ideas man. He is the man who thought of humanising the puritanically austere Field Marshal Montgomery by persuading him to wear a Tank Corps black beret and a sloppy sweater, and to distribute free cigarettes while commanding troops in the Western Desert. Warwick was the first to realise that Britain's main asset is its past. He conceived of a commercial synthetic miniature Merrie England which would exploit the happy bits of the nation's history, and relinquished the project only when Mrs Thatcher decided that Britain, instigator of the Industrial Revolution, should leave manufacturing to other nations, such as Taiwan, and concentrate instead on the service industries, in a country transformed into one great theme park. He masterminded the construction of a replica of the *Mayflower* and the sailing of *Mayflower II* from Plymouth to Plymouth, Massachusetts, where the Pilgrim Fathers landed. He summed up his philosophy in the dictum: 'Enough is not as good as a feast; a feast is better.' To practise what he preached, he often

27

entertained prodigally at the club that he and Dick Brennan had founded on a vision of romantic hindsight. There should have been a club there since the seventeenth century. Why deny that there was?

When I attended a banquet in Harvey's wine cellars on the eve of *Mayflower II*'s voyage across the Atlantic, Dick confessed to me in late-evening conversation that he was sailing as the ship's second cook even though he was not much use in the galley. 'Please don't give me away,' he said. 'If you promise not to mention it to anyone, I'll make you a life member of the club.' The prospect of many years of belonging to a club without having to pay for the privilege was an attractive one. I don't suppose it matters now to reveal that Dick was a noncooking seacook. He pretended to be a cook for the free ride. Warwick didn't mind. He was busy at the time, negotiating exclusive picture rights to the voyage with *Life* magazine and *Paris-Match* simultaneously, an overlapping of interests which caused noisy agitation in a Plymouth hotel for all the rest of that night. But I must not digress.

As I had ascertained by telephone, Warwick and Dick were both in one of the smaller, quieter upstairs bars when I ushered Chesley Brewster into the Wig, as it is known to its habitués. I was pleased to see that a bottle of champagne was already uncorked in an ice bucket on a window table, and there were four glasses.

Introductions were effected and Warwick told our guest some of the history that has accreted to the club since its postwar establishment.

'The Great Fire of 1666 laid waste a lot of the City,' Warwick said. 'Yet this building wasn't even singed.'

Chesley would have been less impressed if Warwick had added that the club's premises had not been built until centuries later.

'Chesley's been telling me about the American Bar Association convention,' I said. 'There are thousands of America's top lawyers here. The best hotels are full of them.'

'Some of us who signed up late have had to take rooms as far away as Bristol and come in on the train every day,' Chesley said. 'I'm fortunate. I'm in Claridge's.'

I saw dollar signs shining in Dick's crafty dark eyes.

'Thousands of you?' he said. 'You couldn't all fit in here at once, Chesley, but I'll tell you what: I'll make you an honorary member as long as you're in town, and you can invite as many friends here as you like.'

'They've got a wonderful program,' I said. 'They're going everywhere – the Palace of Westminster, the Inns of Court. They're going to Runnymede, to see where Magna Carta was signed. And there's to be a garden party at Buckingham Palace. I wish I were a paid-up member of the ABA.'

'I'm surprised you're not,' Warwick exclaimed, coming in on cue. 'You should be. Chesley, Patrick is one of nature's born litigants.'

'That's true,' Dick confirmed. 'He's probably the most litigious person I know. There are barristers across the road who don't understand the law any better than he does.'

In the taxi on the way to drop me in Soho before Chesley went on to Mayfair, he said: 'Pat, I'm grateful for that introduction, and I know my friends will be too. I'm going to see what I can do for you with the chairman of the program committee. Al's a regular guy. Give me a buzz at the hotel in the morning.'

That was how I found myself, a few afternoons later, with Chesley in a Daimler limousine, as long and black and shiny as a hearse, gliding slowly down the Mall. Procuring the invitation, he said, had been 'no sweat'. As we rounded the Queen Victoria Memorial, I felt a sphincteral twinge of anxiety, but the gilt-edged pasteboard was taken with the most casual glance, and soon I was crossing the forecourt of the Palace.

George IV commissioned John Nash to aggrandise the Duke of Buckingham's early eighteenth-century mansion. Direct from his success in designing the Brighton Pavilion, the Regent's fantasy playhouse, with its secret backstairs for amorous trysting, Nash did a good job on improving the King's London residence. No expense was spared. There are probably those who would say that royalty are the world's most expert freeloaders. I admire their skill.

Walking through the grand ivory and gold Bow Room, I was slightly disappointed to see no crested ashtrays suitable for keepsakes. I imagined Her Majesty stowed them away with all the other loose bric-a-brac whenever she was expecting nine thousand guests for tea.

Onward, through the doorway between long, crimson curtains, I came to the West terrace and a flight of wide, shallow stone steps to the vast lawn. As Chesley and I were among the first arrivals, we had time to stroll about unimpeded, exploring a little of the forty-acre garden. It is a big garden in this desirable neighbourhood.

'How much do you figure this would be worth on the open market if Britain became a republic?' he asked.

'Possibly nothing during a civil war,' I replied. Anyway, I liked the garden as it was.

Roses of several colours were in orderly bloom. The herbaceous borders were as beautifully gaudy as a seed catalogue. But whére were the celebrated flamingos? Shouldn't they be wading in the lake? Or was I dreamily confusing this place with the Queen of Hearts' garden in *Alice's Adventures in Wonderland*? Nothing about Buckingham Palace seems quite real.

Perhaps the flamingos had taken refuge in a remote corner behind trees to get away from the music. On a bandstand by the shore of the lake, a military band was playing a medley from *My Fair Lady*. They were smart in their bearskins, scarlet tunics and dark blue trousers, with the sunshine bouncing off their brass buttons and brass instruments.

'Who are they? They're good,' Chesley said.

'The Brigade of Guards. Scarlet plumes – the Coldstream.'

'Shouldn't they be playing marches though?'

'At teatime?'

'It was teatime. The guests were all assembled, milling about, awaiting Her Majesty, her consort and their retinue. A few of the visiting men had hired light grey top hats and morning dress; some of the women had invested in elaborately trimmed, wide-brimmed hats, almost preposterous enough for Royal Ascot, but of course not quite that silly.

Then the Queen and the rest of the royal cortège came into view, gathering the crowd close around them, as a magnet attracts iron filings.

Chesley and I parted company. He joined the throng and I went to the tea tent. I had the large tent almost exclusively to myself. For my own personal record, I ate a dainty cucumber sandwich and a chocolate éclair. My teacup was filled from a hissing chromium-plated urn. The girl who gave me the tea did not know the name of the blend. It seemed to me as good as the Lyons Gold Label tea I drink at home.

It was an ordinary cup of tea. To me, however, it was an achievement, the culmination of a week's exertion. If you want to enquire about future, possibly crashable garden parties at Buckingham Palace, the Palace's telephone number is (071) 930 4832. There's no need to mention my name.

4

TO ease the way into favourable situations, one should make all sorts of contacts, even if they do not all seem attractive themselves. One thing leads to another. I happened to approach Number 10 Downing Street by way of Blackpool.

Blackpool is a seaside place, as the old song says, 'noted for fresh air and fun'. To anyone who has ever attended a Conservative Party annual conference there (or in Brighton or Scarborough), the claim may seem ironic. Delegates spend most of their time in the crowded conference hall and in smoke-filled rooms, discussing the totally unfunny subject of political survival. The beds are hardly ever used for any activity but sleeping.

For all the gloomy forebodings that oppress most of those present, particularly, of course, Members of Parliament unsure that their constituents will give them votes of confidence in the next General Election, there is one major consolation: the expense account. Politicians have ample and wonderfully flexible expense accounts, whatever they say publicly to the contrary. Apart from the basic necessities – transport, room and board – there are legitimate, grey areas less easily defined, most notably 'entertainment'. As a nonpolitician and nonvoter without an expense account, I sometimes overcome my squeamishness about MPs and seek their company.

MPs typically are gregarious extroverts by nature, yet often lonely. They inevitably spend much of their time with other MPs, who are all apparent or potential competitors. No other occupational group is more suspicious. I have learned that generally they welcome anyone who they are sure has no political axe to grind. If they know they are unpopular with their colleagues, or their constituents, or all of them, not an uncommon condition, they are pathetically eager to ingratiate themselves with anyone who seems tolerantly receptive, and to

34

be treated kindly, or at least uncritically, as if they were one's equals. It is the easiest imaginable accomplishment, to snare an MP. I made that discovery in the distant past. When I was living near Broadway (the village in Worcestershire), I was able to get the late Sir Gerald Nabarro, MP, to endorse legislation of interest to a friend of mine (something to do with licensing a London casino), at a cost, I recall of only £10,000 a year for a few years.

In Blackpool, I checked into a small bed-and-breakfast place in a terrace of red-brick houses reminiscent of *Coronation Street*. Only a couple of blocks inland from the seafront carnival known as 'The Golden Mile', the prices were relatively low. From this base, I walked the few hundred yards to the four-star hotel patronised by the leaders of the party and their more affluent acolytes.

Over a cup of ersatz coffee in a bile-green upholstered and grey-pickled-walnut panelled lounge which reeked of the previous evening's cigarettes and the morning's imitation-pine air freshener, I scanned the *Daily Telegraph* for the names of delegates scheduled to speak before lunch.

I came upon precisely the sort of man and cause I was searching for. Sir Romilly Gascoigne, MP (Con, Devonport East), was to speak in support of his own resolution to privatise the Royal Navy, in order to finance some badly needed new ships (or words to that effect). I had heard that Sir Romilly was a man of immense inherited wealth; he had been knighted for services to industry (contributions to party funds); however, it was doubtful that the proposal he was expounding would endear him to sentimental fellow members or to many of the traditionalists in his maritime constituency. His portrait, one column wide in the paper, showed him to be a bald man with a neat, grey moustache, an apoplectic complexion and hyperthyroid eyes bulging with fanaticism. Perfect.

Having made sure that he was registered in the hotel, I repaired to the bar, where I occupied a stool close to the entrance. There was no need to subject myself to the boredom of going to the hall and listening to his speech. I felt certain that immediately after the ordeal he would come straight to the bar. He did.

'Congratulations!' I said, surprising him with the compliment and a large brandy and ginger, which had been made ready in

35

anticipation. He took it gratefully with a trembling hand and had a good, restorative gulp before speaking.

'You were in the hall?'

'Not actually down in the main body of the audience,' I said, suggesting that it had been from a superior viewpoint that I had admired his performance. 'What impressed me was that you said what you had to say.'

'You don't think I was overemphatic?'

'How could you have been?' I said, giving him an encouraging pat on the shoulder. He drank some more and seemed to relax.

'I don't think we've met,' he said.

'No. I've just come from London, as an observer.'

'From Central Office?'

I chuckled good-humouredly at the very notion of Tory headquarters.

'Hardly,' I said. I winked, implying at least an influential, secret think-tank. 'But of course I am very interested in the formulation of ideas as such. I believe I have a pretty sound grasp of what you are and what you must be up against. "A prophet in his own country" sort of thing, eh?'

'It's a pleasure to meet someone who is willing to try to understand,' he said, indicating to the barman with a small, circular motion of a forefinger that replenishment was due.

'I'd like to hear in detail your plan for privatisation of the Navy,' I said. 'Some of our greatest successes were achieved during the era of privateers. The Navy today is of great symbolic importance – too important for the inefficiency of state ownership. I suppose Telecom must have inspired you.'

'But there is opposition,' he admitted, momentarily sagging.

'Of course there is!' I exclaimed, giving him a heartier fraternal pat that almost caused him to lose his equilibrium. 'You are a man ahead of your time. The rest of us are somewhere quite different. We'll have to catch up with you. When I return to London, I'll be seeing some people. A word to the wise. I wish you weren't so busy. We should have a talk. I'd like to hear your ideas about the Army and Air Force.'

'There's nothing this afternoon I can't get out of,' he assured me. 'Why don't we have lunch?'

I frowned at my watch, stared at the ceiling for a moment or two, as if making important calculations, and then generously smiled at him.

'Oh, all right,' I conceded. 'Why not? A working lunch. There's no time like the present.'

The saying 'There is no such thing as a free lunch' is clever but could be counterproductive. A wise guy might say that pretending to listen attentively to a twisted megalomaniac and occasionally murmuring sympathetically 'uh-huh?' or 'mmm...' is paying a price; but, even if it is, it's a small price to pay for pâté de foie gras, turtle soup, lobster thermidor and salad, Grand Marnier soufflé and a Brie close to the point of ripeness, soft and almost, but not quite, runny. And I've always been partial to a Puligny-Montrachet of a better-than-average year.

We parted late that afternoon on the most cordial terms. We exchanged telephone numbers and he made me promise to call him in London.

After a decent delay, I telephoned his apartment in the Barbican. He invited me to meet him the following day at the House of Commons. He was waiting in the Central Lobby when I arrived, and he beamed so radiantly that I was quite sorry I had forgotten most of our luncheon conversation. Luckily, it soon became apparent that my little lapse was of no consequence.

We took tea on the Terrace, overlooking the river, which, glittering in the sunshine, appeared less like mulligatawny soup than in recent years. Pollution can be cured. Buoyed up by a sense of optimistic wellbeing, I was glad to give him the advice I had devised.

'What I feel you need,' I told him, 'is a place in the Cabinet. The Ministry of Defence would provide the right platform for the enactment of your reforms. The present minister doesn't seem to be getting much done.'

'I'm so glad that's your opinion,' Sir Romilly said, silently striking a palm with a loosely clenched fist. 'I think you're absolutely spot-on there. But how – '

'Ah!' I interrupted, enjoying a sense of strengthening dominance. I wagged an admonitory finger. 'That's the nub, isn't it? You must get closer to the Prime Minister. There's always room in the party coffers.' I lifted my chin challengingly. 'How about it, Romilly? Have you got what it takes? The way to the party's heart, you know, is through its coffers.'

'Do you really – '

'I certainly do.' I had looked him up in *Who's Who*. 'You could sell a few hundred acres of the Wiltshire estate, if necessary. But you shouldn't ask for your peerage yet. At first you must make your mark in the lower house. And of course a ministerial portfolio would be useful.'

'Yes, I see.'

'Write to the Prime Minister. Tell her frankly what you have in mind. Suggest that you call on her for a chat. And suggest that you and she have your photograph taken, shaking hands. She likes being photographed shaking hands. A display of solidarity would be helpful all round. I know the right photographer. If you give me notice, I may be able to come along myself.'

'Would you?' Sir Romilly said, his eyes ablaze with sincere lust for office.

I was permitted to accompany the photographer to Number 10 as his assistant. To look the part, I wore a denim jacket and tennis shoes and carried a leather gadget bag and a couple of Nikons and a Hasselblad slung from my neck. Cameras are the modern world's most potent credentials, valid for entrée into every inner sanctum. This was back in the days when it seemed as if Mrs Thatcher's tenure of office was to be permanent; but she, being more astute than most of her supporters, already foresaw the hostile graffiti on the wall, and was doing her best to ingratiate herself with the fickle public. She apparently thought that enlarging her bouffant blonde coiffure and smiling kindly into lenses might prolong her term of leadership.

Sir George Downing, a diplomat with a keen eye on the main chance, speculatively constructed the short row of houses in the street named after him between Whitehall and Horse Guards Road. Completed in the 1680s, they justified his optimism when George II decided in 1731 that one of the houses would be fit to accommodate his Prime Minister, Sir Robert Walpole. Mrs Thatcher, the first woman to succeed to the residence, says she brightened the décor of the flat – especially the kitchen – above the offices. Having been brought up over a shop, she said she felt at home in Number 10.

I had visited the house on and off since the time of Sir Anthony Eden, as he was then. Perhaps in tribute to the ancestral Eden who governed Maryland when it was a colony, Sir Anthony used to make excellent dry martini cocktails. If Number 10's old walls could talk they would probably mention a lot of other stimulating refreshments that have been served by susbequent prime ministers.

'It's really quite a small house,' Sir Romilly commented, perhaps attempting to disguise his awe. He had never been invited there before, and some millionaire politicians are more impressionable than others but hate to admit the fact.

We passed the modest black front door and were admitted to the hall. We had been instructed to arrive at 10 am, an hour before the photo session was due to begin. The photograper had demanded that long to set up his floodlights, spotlights and aluminium umbrellas. The carpet was traversed by an entanglement of snake-like cables. When all the auxiliary equipment was installed and checked and checked again and a Contaflex was attached to his tripod, he began taking readings from his light meter close to Sir Romilly's face, which was sweating in the heat of the lights, augmented by premonitory stage fright.

The Prime Minister emerged from her downstairs sitting room at exactly 11 o'clock. Her dress was a snappy blue number, with shoes to match. Her highly inflated, platinum-blonde hairdo enabled her to tower above her nervous guest.

'Well, let's get on with it,' she said to the photographer.

He switched on a blaze of white lights, thus simultaneously switching on her smile, the first-magnitude one used for photo opportunities. She told Sir Romilly where to stand. Then, in the usual way, she moved a foot or two upstage, and limply grasped his hand while she continued to look straight into the camera.

'Let me know when you're going to start,' she said.

'Now, if I may, Prime Minister,' the photographer said, in an uncharacteristically meek tone, already having succumbed to the woman's dreadful power. She quickly licked her lips, just like a Page Three model, a real pro, preparing a glistening pout, and again switched on the smile.

As the camera repeatedly clicked and whined and the photographer kept saying, 'That's great, Prime Minister! Yes, terrific! Another of those! Fantastic!', I knew I could safely leave them at it for at least a few minutes.

I recognised a bemedalled, uniformed inner doorman who

had been there, seeing prime ministers come and go, for many years.

'I'm just going back to the toilet,' I said. 'OK?'

He responded with the lightest flicker of a wink. He smiled.

'Certainly, sir. There's plenty of that stuff in the usual place.'

'Good man!' He was a nice fellow. We had had drinks together more than once across Whitehall.

I hurried along a short corridor, turned right, and there it was, sure enough, a stack of brown-paper packages on top of a low bookcase. I had no need to go any farther; I didn't want the loo. In the present régime, I thought rather bitterly, one could die of thirst in that house.

When I returned to the hall/studio, the shoot was still in progress, of course. As with most other eminent photographers, my friend, unlike Cartier-Bresson, didn't feel he could count on getting satisfactory photographs, even when posed for, unless, unlike Cartier-Bresson, he took several hundreds of them. Fortunately, the Prime Minister appeared to be enjoying herself. She had already started telling the photographer what to do.

Confident that I was unnoticed, I slipped my package into the gadget bag I had brought with me. I whispered in the photographer's ear that I was going ahead and asked him to tell Sir Romilly, who now looked happy, that I'd be in touch some time. I told the friendly doorman that I looked forward to seeing him in the pub as soon as he got off for lunch.

Once I had obtained the first drink of the day, I took out the package and eagerly tore off its wrappings.

Ah! It contained what I wanted, 480 sheets of 24-pound-stock, creamy white paper, heavily embossed at the top with the royal coat of arms, in black, and the words, like a spendid fanfare of trumpets, THE PRIME MINISTER.

I don't use Number 10 writing paper often, but several years had elapsed since I had managed to pick up the last ream and my stock was low.

Larceny? Come, come. That's an ugly word. It's perfectly all right to take a little souvenir from an institution one admires, especially if it is financed by the taxpayers.

I sometimes find the paper useful.

5

HAVING spent some time in the United States of America almost every year of my adult life, I have been able to visit every region of the country in all seasons. I have enjoyed almost all of it, almost always. It is a good country to be a citizen of. With a valid United States passport you can usually get through customs at JFK without a strip search. Miami nowadays is a bit more difficult.

New York is richly fruitful throughout the year. The city does not close down annually, as conventional Parisians feel that Paris should, in August. Many New Yorkers of means do try to get out of town during the steamiest weeks of the summer. Many don't. Strange to say, from the point of view of a visitor who seeks the most for the least, New York in late summer, climatically at its worst, can be in some ways at its best. People who elect, or who are compelled, to stay there at that time are often clinically bored and exceptionally approachable. It's a time that may be recommended to neophytes.

One August Sunday afternoon, I was sitting alone at a table for two in the sombrely masculine basement dining room of the Lotos Club. Situated on East Sixty-sixth Street just off Fifth Avenue, the club is eminently respectable, though ex-President Nixon was a member and possibly still is. His disgrace was not of long duration. The late President Eisenhower was also a member; perhaps he nominated Nixon. I was staying there because of the club's respectability (the club had an arrangement of reciprocal privileges with an equally dull men's club I belonged to in London), and because the Lotos is considerably cheaper than a good hotel.

The cool air smelled of dusty air conditioning and stale Republicanism. At 2.15, I had eaten enough of my overcooked liver and bacon with mashed potatoes and peas and was

42

strenuously working on digesting them, while staring at a wedge of apple pie, considering the possibility of insinuating a fork into the sodden cardboard crust, and, at the same time, trying to read a postmodernist's analysis of Arnold Bennett's *The Old Wives' Tale* in the *New York Times Book Review*. There was nobody else in the room but an elderly Afro-American waiter, an Uncle Remus figure, leaning against a jamb of the kitchen door and obviously wishing he was somewhere else, and an even more elderly pink-faced man in a charcoal-grey suit who was sitting, like me, on his own, despondently chewing food he didn't want.

I saw him crook a finger at the waiter and I feared that my solitude would soon be total. But no: the waiter came over to me and said that Colonel Symington invited me to join him at his table for coffee.

'Quiet here at this time of the year,' he said, half complaining, half apologising. 'You're a guest, aren't you?'

I introduced myself.

'Room all right?'

'Yes, fine, thank you.'

'Wretched place really. Convenient, of course, but nobody here. Nothing to do. Would you care for a brandy?'

I cared for three of them, quite large ones, in balloon glasses. He wouldn't allow me to pay for any of them.

'You can buy me a drink the next time I'm in London,' he said in that cordial, vague manner that people assume when pledging eternal friendship with fellow passengers aboard a cruise ship.

'I say,' he said, sounding more English and genially Blimpish as the afternoon wore on (he had served as a military attaché at the American Embassy in Grosvenor Square and spent many happy hours at the Naval & Military Club [the In & Out]), 'if you're bored absolutely rigid, there's a do at the English-Speaking Union this afternoon. Only a few blocks from here. A short lecture – it makes people feel they're improving their minds. Then perhaps sherry. Usually a few reasonably interesting members and guests to chat with. I myself won't be going – time for my siesta – but you can say I sent you, if you wish.'

Adhering to my policy of exposing myself to as many possibilities as I can, I accepted his kind offer.

Less than half an hour later I was sitting on a flimsy cane chair, among several rows of chairs of which fewer than half were occupied, in a dim, curtained drawing room, struggling to stay awake as I watched a film on the stained glass of Wells Cathedral. The lady who had made the film, a Bostonian I guessed, was present beside the projector to give us a running commentary. As stained glass does not move, she had imparted motion by swinging the camera to and fro in continuous panoramic sweeps.

'Notice the lovely geometrical tracery in the windows of the Lady Chapel,' she said. 'Oh, dear. Perhaps I should go back and show that again. It was quick, wasn't it?' But as nobody in the small audience expressed any desire for repetition, she did not bother to rewind the film.

At last the screen went brightly blank and there was a conclusive flapping noise.

'Well, that's it,' she admitted.

Somebody switched on the room's main lights. There was a flutter of polite hand clapping, some of it unfortunately muted by gloves.

'If there are any questions?'

'I toured the West Country of Britain in 1947,' a man said. 'It was one of the coldest winters they've ever had over there. There was rationing.'

'Wells Cathedral isn't as big as Durham,' a woman said.

'Those statues along the West façade are in very bad shape,' commented a veteran sightseer who wanted her experience credited. 'When I was there, they said all that old sculpture was going to be restored. It was originally multicoloured, you know. What happened to that plan?'

'It's long-term,' the lecturer said. 'Funds are needed.'

'Thank you, Dr Gillespie,' the chairman of the day said. 'We are all very grateful for that fascinating peek at old Wells Cathedral.' There was a little more applause. 'Tea will be in the other lounge.'

My heart felt like a chestful of cold suet as I followed the murmurous group of matrons in hats, with a couple of walking-wounded men in tow, across the hall into a similar room of flowery chintz and pale watercolours. I might as well hang about until the end. You can't win if you don't play.

It was lucky I stayed. It was over a cup of Earl Grey and a

brownie (no sherry) that I met Mrs Stanmore-Woolley, who told me all about the Versailles Ball at the Waldorf-Astoria Hotel.

The Versailles Ball is one of the numerous major charitable festivities that enrich the New York year as truffles enrich pâté. Now that *le tout New York* has been increased from Mrs Astor's arbitrary 400 to as many as the traffic will bear – an apparently unlimited number – women prepared to spend large sums of money to be categorised as ladies invest in heavily publicised, if not quite public, displays of extravagant charity, usually enacted in the ballrooms of the grander Manhattan hotels. Millions of dollars are collected, and, after administrative overheads have been taken care of, some of the proceeds trickle down to causes such as the Save the Platypus Fund, the Twilight Home for Senior Tennis Players and research into the latest fashionable disease. The social ladder thus has become an express escalator.

Mrs Stanmore-Woolley told me that the Versailles Ball was a recently established event of paramount importance in the New York social calendar, superseding the old April in Paris Ball, which used to be autumn's most scintillating exhibition of conspicuous consumption. It is already impossible to say which public relations consultant came up with Versailles, a creative concept lost in the mists of novelty.

In this age of perestroika, giantesses of the garment industry, vying for charitable primacy, have proved it is all right to give parties with a Russian theme. One may offer vodka and caviar et cetera without any risk of political odium, so long as the cabaret features, say, the Kirov Ballet or the Red Army Choir, which has been greatly augmented with so many singers back from their success with the Warsaw Pact that several road companies of the virile choristers are available for hire in the West. Mrs H. Pierrepoint Frick effectively defused all possible carping comment on her big Glastnost Jamboree when she distributed, as table favours for the ladies, miniature 22-carat balalaikas, and, for the gentlemen, traditional gold Sputnik cigar lighters.

The Versailles, however, though not the newest annual ball, still has a certain cachet, a *je ne sais quoi* of pre-Revolutionary France, which appeals to subscribers with conservative aspirations. Also, perpetuating the past is ostentatiously more expensive than conforming with the present. The Versailles décor and furnishings cost a pretty penny. As Mrs Stanmore-Woolley coyly divulged, the subscription for a table of eight at the banquet, cabaret and dance had set her back eight thousand dollars.

'I'd love for you to come,' she said. 'As my guest. I need a gentleman to balance my seating plan.'

She was a blue-rinsed, stout party of advanced maturity who looked as if her seating plan had been balanced long ago. Somehow during our one-sided conversation the fact emerged that she had been married to an extremely successful English dealer in soy bean futures who had burnt out early. Her occasional attendance at cultural get-togethers at the English-Speaking Union, she explained, was a sort of memorial tribute to him.

'He was very dear,' she whimpered with a brave little smile. 'You don't really remind me of him, except that you are English, aren't you?'

I smiled modestly.

'That's a Savile Row suit, isn't it?' she said. 'Monty had all his suits made there.' As a matter of fact, I got it from a little man in Petticoat Lane. 'Well, I mean,' she added, 'I can see you're not Eurotrash.'

Touched by her loyal, sentimental regard for her late husband and favourably impressed by her plain black Chanel suit, her Aztec silver and turquoise brooch and her enthusiastic bid for my company, I accepted her invitation without further ado.

'It's black tie,' she said. 'And I prefer black tuxedos, don't you?' I was glad, as I did not own a white dinner jacket at the time. Her sartorial orthodoxy put paid to those canards put about by the likes of Evelyn Waugh, whose ear trumpet failed to pick up authentic American vibes. If you believed people like him you would believe that American men on formal evenings must wear Black Watch cummerbunds and buttonhole flowers made of maroon fluffy imitation silk.

The Waldorf ballroom on the night looked right out of this century, as Peggy Guggenheim might have put it. The colour scheme was grey-blue, white and silver. Banners emblazoned with fleurs-de-lis were festooned in loops along the walls, with swags of lilies in the corners and gardenias in silver bowls on the tables. Specially commissioned murals depicted the splendid château, the fountains, the symmetrical gardens and the Avenue des États-Unis.

'*Très chic*, don't you agree?' Mrs Stanmore-Woolley rhetorically opined.

'Very Louis Quatorzeish!' confirmed a middle-aged albino elf with acne scars and long, sparse white hair, on her left. 'Quite divine, Amanda darling!' She had put me on her right, but I was unable to match his praise. There were two young women, shinily brushed chestnut and titian, and one no longer young, whose face had been surgically lifted so tight that she could hardly open her mouth, all three exquisitely coiffured, be-jewelled and gowned, chartreuse, coffee and oyster respectively. And, of course, two more males, one who could well have been a 4-F matinée idol of the war years who had gone beyond seed, and a man probably in his late thirties with short yellow curls and a deep tan who looked as though he regularly worked out in a health club for aesthetic reasons and might model ski-wear.

The menu was superb, featuring two of the specialities of Trois Marches, the best restaurant in Versailles, France – *flan chaud de foie gras aux huitres et écrevisses* and *canard de Challans au vinaigre de cidre et miel* – worthy of a detour. Alternatively, for weight watchers, there was a choice of *crêpes au fromage Kraft* or nothing. The wines were outstanding and abundant. Guests who didn't want them were offered carcino-genic mineral water and diet Pepsi.

The conversation was recycled gossip from *W* and *People*, with occasional more earnest references to *Time* and *Dun & Bradstreet*.

A soprano diva from the Metropolitan Opera began the enter-tainment with a dramatic rendition of 'I Love Paris'. During the applause, I whispered an inaudible excuse in Mrs Stanmore-Woolley's – Amanda's – diamond-studded ear and tiptoed away fast.

After a refreshing cold wash, I wandered about for a while, eventually coming upon a champagne bar, pleasantly secluded on the far side of the dance floor.

'Hi, Pat! Couldn't take it, huh?' said the ski-wear model, whose appetite for the wines at the table had exceeded even my own.

'You beat me to it,' I said, raising in recognition of his superior

agility the glass that the attentive bartender had promptly filled.
'Cheers, Mr Black!'

'Rudi,' he corrected me. His eyes were slightly glazed and his
enunciation was less than a hundred per cent clear. 'Rudi Black,
né Schwartzenburger, but some people had a problem with
that. My agent says I ought to go all the way – drop Rudi – call
myself Rod. He says Rod has a good, hard thrust to it. Whaddya
think, Pat?'

'Your agent says?'

'Yeah, my agent. I like him to make my key decisions. Don't
you have an agent? Or are you trying to cling to your amateur
status?'

His laugh lacked warmth.

'Are you an actor, Rudi?'

'Aw, Pat. Don't bullshit me. I'm a guest, like you. I'm registered
with Guests International – best agency in town. Ask anyone.
Hostesses have had PR for years. Why shouldn't we guests have
a little boost when we need it?'

In spite of the present slight fuzziness around the edges, his
words were spoken with the resonant euphony of Coast-to-Coast
Network Standard American. I deduced that he had been paying
devout attention to America's leading news presenters since his
early childhood or he had had a recent crash course in showbiz
elocution. When he opened his mouth, I noticed that his teeth
were immaculately capped.

The United States is often one step or more ahead of Europe
in commercial innovation. Guests International! How times have
changed since Henry James wrote of American innocence and
European worldliness! I confessed to Rudi frankly that I had
never heard of Guests International. But the name had a ring to
it.

'Celebrities are celebrities,' he pointed out, 'and hostesses
want them. There's always a place at these affairs for an Andy
Warhol, a Duke of Bedford, a Mick Jagger; even, on another
level, a Taki Theodoracopolous. But, to fill in, there's a constant
demand for presentable single men of all ages, including a fair
number of straights. You know?'

I nodded and plied him with what Max Beerbohm called 'the
spur of silence'. Rudi continued:

'That's where people like me can score. There's a lot of

competition, but fortunately that includes all the undesirables that come here like flies around a honey pot. Even in this age of universal democratic reform, there are still parasites who expect hospitality in the name of White Russia. Their grandfathers were Paris taxi drivers. There are pretenders to non-existent thrones. Inexperienced hostesses will go for a Prince of Albania and a row of phony medals. I've seen a guy with a *monocle*, for Chrissake. It's a sellers' market for normals.'

He held out his empty glass and it was refilled.

'We're properly organised now, some of us, on a businesslike basis.'

'You're being paid to be here tonight?'

'Sure. Mrs Stanmore-Woolley pays top dollar. What's wrong with that? When I first came to New York – never call it 'The Big Apple', unless you want to sound like you're from Squareville, Iowa – I tried to get by on presents. You can do that, if you're lucky. One nice old lady left me a Patek Philippe watch after I'd sat through a whole bunch of gruesome dinners in Sutton Place. It paid six months' rent for a warehouse pad in the East Village. But there's a downside. I once thought I'd hit the jackpot – a Fabergé Easter egg. What a bummer! A fake. An appraiser at Christie's said it wasn't worth much more than a chocolate one. Me, I'm a believer in security, thanks a lot. I want more than peanut butter and jelly sandwiches.'

'But how could you achieve that?'

He grimaced smugly and spilled some champagne down his shirtfront.

'A top agent. Thass the secret. Sam Rathbone took me on as one of his first clients. You've heard of him, haven't you?'

I couldn't suppress a snort of laughter. I knew about several of his get-richer-quick schemes.

'I seem to remember a scandal about an artificial insemination clinic.'

'No scandal, Pat. He got out of that as clean as a whistle. Anyway, he saw my advertisement in the personals in the *Village Voice*, offering myself as an escort. He got in touch. He said I'd given him an idea. What you *call* a product, he said, is as important as what the product is. 'Escort' had taken on a slimeball connotation. Escort equals gigolo, is the way people think – equals prostitute. Gigolos afraid their charms are fading often panic and marry for money. Escort services are out, Sam said; we should talk guest. He charges twenty per cent, but he's worth it.'

'That's almost as much as art dealers take.'

'Yes, Pat, true. But, as Sam says, it's better to have eighty per cent of something than a hundred per cent of nothing, and I know what it's like to have a nothing week. Right?'

'Right. I know what that's like too.'

'He invested in me,' Rudi said. 'He said for optimum results I should get some cosmopolitan polish. He fixed me up with a voice coach and an etiquette adviser. He made a deal with a travel agent and sent me on a quick European tour – the places that matter, Venice, Monte Carlo, Gstaad. Credentials mean a whole new ball game: Sam was able to get me the best bookings. He got me on the jet circuit. When someone like Bubbles Rand or Mimi Zeitgeist throws a big wingding over in the Seychelles or London, England, or somewhere, they send me an air ticket. Sometimes, for a gang of us, a private plane. You have to watch yourself, of course. I've heard of people, naming no names, who have been asked to carry a small package with them, if you know what I mean. There was one case recently where an acquaintance of mine had to fly to Madrid in a clown costume, would you believe. Customs made him take off the round, red rubber nose, and of course it was full of coke. He's still in the slammer. They say Spanish slammers are nearly as bad as the Turkish ones.'

'I think perhaps I'd better be getting back to the table,' I said. He yawned.

'Mrs Stanmore-Woolley doesn't go for disco music. I'm going to have another glass.'

Rudi apparently wanted to brag some more, and I was quite curious about his operation, even though I had no intention of turning pro.

'Once you make the big time as a name guest with media recognition, there's a lot of pressure,' he said, 'and a lot of rewards. Like top golfers and other leading sport personalities, some of us get sponsors for endorsements.

'For instance,' he went on, 'the American Tobacco Federation has me on retainer. Everyone thinks I smoke nonstop but they can see I'm in great shape. The Federation's spending zillions these days to counter all the knocking. All I have to do is smoke cigarettes at functions like this, and make sure I have a cigarette in my hand whenever pictures are being taken. Haven't you ever wondered why there are so many old movies on TV? The Federation has something to do with that. Payola, Pat. The stars of those romantic musical comedies of the nineteen-thirties and forties were always lighting up. In dramas too. After permissiveness came in and before the anti-smoking propaganda, you'd always see the happy couple puffing cigarettes at the end of every bedroom scene. When I think of Lauren Bacall I want a cigarette.'

Mentioning her name made him produce a gold cigarette case.

'The Old Tavistock bourbon people pay me fifteen grand a year and expenses to name their brand every time I call for a drink in a smart bar. I don't always *drink* it – it's mostly neutral spirits that could burn a hole in your gut – but I am often heard calling for it.'

'There's a lot of fantasy going about. An epidemic.'

'It's a science! And a rat race too, I admit. Where's Dr Feelgood when we need him?' A morose shadow seemed to darken his face for a moment. 'There are times, Pat, between you and me, when I feel I could use a strong amphetamine cocktail laced with vitamin E and steroids. These glitterati can suck the marrow out of your bones. There are mornings when I wouldn't mind retiring and settling down in Bucks County with a nice, quiet heiress.'

'You'll be all right, Rudi!' I lied. 'Let's go back. They must miss you. Do it for Sam.'

'Sure!' he said, clenching his jaws like an old trouper. 'For Sam!'

'There you are, boys!' said Mrs Stanmore-Woolley, welcoming us to the table. 'Isn't the music just too awful? But I've arranged for a photographer to come over in a few minutes to shoot some candids for *Vogue*. We must all be very nice to him. He's a friend of Andy's, but you know how cruel photographers can be in the darkroom if they're upset.'

'Cigarette?' Rudi kept enquiring, passing around his case.

I was pleased to be a free, independent amateur.

The young woman with titian hair and the gown of coffee-coloured lace (*café au lait*) was becoming more and more attractive. I happened to be between marriages, so, at the end of the evening – to tell the truth, a good bit before the end – we went back to her place.

6

LATE the next morning, I was lying, almost floating, in a deep, hot bath, inhaling the sweet fumes of lavender gel, half-listening to a Chopin prelude and half-reminiscing, when I was galvanised by the mechanical scream of an electric coffee grinder.

I found, in the mirrored cabinet above the basin, one of those disposable guest toothbrushes, which, as a disposable guest, I felt qualified to use. The toothpaste pump dispensed a ribbon striped red and white that tasted of mint. I also found a disposable guest razor and a canister of lemon-and-lime shaving foam, my favourite flavour. By the time I had blinked away the Murine and cleared my eyes, I felt remarkably well, and I noticed gratefully that my appetite was in good working order.

As I closed the cabinet door, I saw beside it a long sheet of paper Scotch-taped to the pale peach wall, a list, neatly typed in word-processor sanserif letters that looked like a message from Mission Control. It is a list I learned to value highly. I urge you to keep it for reference if you wish to derive the maximum benefits from New York. I am glad to be able to reproduce it here:

NATIONAL HOLIDAYS OF MEMBER STATES

1 January	Cuba, Haiti, Sudan
4 January	Myanmar
13 January	Togo
26 January	Australia, India
4 February	Sri Lanka
6 February	New Zealand
7 February	Grenada
11 February	Iran (Islamic Republic of)

18 February	Gambia
22 February	Saint Lucia
23 February	Brunei Darussalam, Guyana
25 February	Kuwait
27 February	Dominican Republic
3 March	Morocco
6 March	Ghana
12 March	Mauritius
17 March	Ireland
20 March	Tunisia
23 March	Pakistan
25 March	Greece
26 March	Bangladesh
4 April	Hungary, Senegal
16 April	Denmark
17 April	Democratic Kampuchea, Syrian Arab Republic
18 April	Zimbabwe
26 April	United Republic of Tanzania
27 April	Sierra Leone, Afghanistan
29 April	Japan
30 April	Netherlands, Israel
9 May	Czechoslovakia
15 May	Paraguay
17 May	Norway
25 May	Cameroon
31 May	Argentina, Jordan
1 June	Samoa
2 June	Italy
5 June	Seychelles
6 June	Sweden
7 June	Chad
9 June	United Kingdom of Great Britain & Northern Ireland
10 June	Portugal
12 June	Philippines
17 June	Iceland
23 June	Luxembourg
25 June	Mozambique
26 June	Madagascar

27 June	Djibouti
30 June	Zaire
1 July	Burundi, Canada, Rwanda
4 July	United States of America
5 July	Cape Verde, Venezuela
6 July	Comoros, Malawi
7 July	Solomon Islands
10 July	Bahamas
11 July	Mongolia
12 July	São Tomé e Principe
14 July	France
17 July	Iraq
20 July	Colombia
21 July	Belgium
22 July	Poland
23 July	Egypt
26 July	Liberia, Maldives
28 July	Peru
30 July	Vanuatu
4 August	Burkina-Faso
6 August	Bolivia, Jamaica
9 August	Singapore
10 August	Ecuador
15 August	Congo
17 August	Gabon, Indonesia
23 August	Romania
25 August	Uruguay
31 August	Malaysia, Trinidad & Tobago
1 September	Libyan Arab Jamahiriva
2 September	Viet Nam
3 September	Qatar
6 September	Swaziland
7 September	Brazil
9 September	Bulgaria
12 September	Ethiopia
15 September	Costa Rica, El Salvador, Guatemala, Honduras, Nicaragua
16 September	Mexico, Papua New Guinea
18 September	Chile
19 September	Saint Kitts-Nevis

21 September	Belize, Malta
22 September	Mali
23 September	Saudi Arabia
24 September	Guinea-Bissau
26 September	Yemen
30 September	Botswana
1 October	China, Cyprus, Nigeria
2 October	Guinea
4 October	Lesotho
7 October	German Democratic Republic
9 October	Uganda
10 October	Fiji
12 October	Equatorial Guinea, Spain
14 October	Democratic Yemen
21 October	Somalia
24 October	Zambia
26 October	Austria
27 October	Saint Vincent & the Grenadines
29 October	Turkey
1 November	Algeria, Antigua & Barbuda
3 November	Dominica, Panama
7 November	Byelorussian Soviet Socialist Republic, Ukranian Soviet Socialist Republic, Union of Soviet Socialist Republics
11 November	Angola
18 November	Oman
22 November	Lebanon
25 November	Surinam
28 November	Mauritania
29 November	Albania, Yugoslavia
30 November	Barbados, Benin
1 December	Central African Republic
2 December	Lao People's Democratic Republic, United Arab Emirates
5 December	Thailand
6 December	Finland
7 December	Ivory Coast
12 December	Kenya
16 December	Bahrain
17 December	Bhutan

18 December	Niger
23 December	Japan
28 December	Nepal

There was a knock on the bathroom door.

'Are you still alive in there?' the young woman wanted to know. 'Breakfast is getting cold.'

I went out wearing a towel. She threw me a man's navy-blue silk dressing gown.

There was a table by French windows overlooking a small patio enclosed by white-painted brick walls. A circular pool with lilies was set in the middle of grey flagstones. In a dark green wooden tub a flowerless plant was wilting. Inside the house, though, the temperature was comfortably cool.

She was already dressed, in faded blue jeans and a pale brown Small's Paradise T-shirt. The titian hair was tied in a girlish ponytail. She was standing beside the table, pouring coffee. It smelled like very good coffee.

'My name's Carmen,' she reminded me.

'Of course,' I agreed, sitting down.

'Eggs Benedict, if that's all right.'

'Fine.'

The papaya juice was ice-cold.

'Those long beige capsules are B-12,' she pointed out.

'Good idea.'

There was some coarse wholewheat toast and Oxford marmalade. Halfway through the second cup of coffee, I said: 'Very nice place you have here. Where exactly are we?'

'Tudor City Place. Just off Fortieth Street. The UN is just across the Plaza there.'

'Oh, I see. You work at the United Nations. I was wondering about the list in the bathroom.'

Carmen laughed indulgently.

'No, I don't work there. That's my party list. The Versailles thing was an off night.' She smiled and politely added, 'Up to a point. I was there to help out poor old Amanda. She's a cousin of my mother's. What was your excuse?'

I hemmed and hawed, as I didn't feel able at that early hour and on such brief acquaintance to propound the philosophy of my perennial quest for free food and drink of superior quality.

Going back a little in the conversation, I asked: 'Your party list?'

'Members of the UN give some of the most interesting, most lavish parties in New York – some of the best anywhere, I imagine. In the UN missions to headquarters, we have a microcosm of Planet Earth: all the peoples, with all their various cultures and customs, and some of the wildest cocktails and canapés you ever tasted. Let me show you something. Bring your cup.'

I followed her to the sitting room, where we had spent a pleasant time the night before, in front of the log fire. In one corner of the room, previously unnoticed by me, there was a study area, a large desk, two walls of bookshelves and one of those noticeboards which methodical Americans often use to pin up memoranda to themselves. In the middle of the board there was a National Geographic map, a large-scale Mercator projection of the world, in which tiny flags of several colours had been stuck widespread.

'See!' she said. 'My collection of countries up to now. Each flag represents a party, and the colours are my own qualitative ratings code for future reference. This is only my second year, but you can see I've been busy. Within two or three more years, I should have done the whole world, and then I'll be selective.' She looked as proud as fanatic collectors of postage stamps displaying their albums. 'Do you know the present size of UN membership?'

I had to confess that I did not. I had lost count many years ago, when the total exceeded a hundred.

'It's a hundred and sixty plus,' she said exultantly. 'It stuck for a while at a hundred and fifty-nine, but, of course, recent fragmentation of the Sovet Union and its satellites has created quite a few new states. I understand that Belugastan is having its inaugural Independence Day bash next week. The more, the merrier! This new proliferation suits me fine, needless to say. I love the Eastern bloc. Most of their delegates are so glad to be here, they blow great party.'

'Hmmm,' I commented, moving closer to the map, to identify some remote, obscure countries. 'There were some names on your list I'd never heard of. Where's Comoros? Where are São Tomé and Principe?'

She looked pleased, even a little smug.

'Comoros is one of the smaller republics in the Organisation,' she said in the rather condescending, didactic tone that I associated with kindergarten and Downing Street. 'There,' she said. With an elegant fingernail, she indicated three dots, a group of islands between Mozambique and Madagascar, in the Indian Ocean. 'HE – His Excellency M. Amini Ali Moumin, their Ambassador Extraordinary and Plenipotentiary, Permanent Representative to the United Nations – is a sweetie-pie. And I have the greatest respect for Madame Moumin: a charmer. Their Independence Day was 6 July. I've given it a gold flag; that's tops. I may be wrong, but I think I'd always be welcome at Mutsamudu. That's on Anjouan. They say it would be a lovely place for a winter holiday, if you took a villa close to the beach, of course, on the windward side. The people are Muslims but very tolerant. I'm seriously thinking about going one day.'

'And São Tomé? That sounds exotic.'

Carmen seemed delighted.

'Now that's *small*!' she exclaimed with a giggle of triumph. 'That must be the smallest one of all. The Holy See would be smaller, but it's only an observer. São Tomé and Principe are among my favourites. I love small. It's funny, how you picked on two of the members I like so much. São Tomé's over on the other side of Africa – there, right smack dab on the equator, in the Gulf of Guinea. Ana Maria, the Ambassador's wife, is a very, very nice lady. I don't have any plans to visit the islands in the near future though. They may not be the most convenient places for shopping. Well, if you had to, I guess you could run over to Libreville, in Gabon. As it happens, the Gabon party was a couple of weeks ago. Not bad: I'd give it six out of ten. And you've missed São Tomé's Independence Day; that was also in July. You have a long wait till next time.'

My ears pricked up at the implication that I could simply drop in on São Tomé's Independence Day party next summer if I was in town.

'That all sounds good,' I said. 'What's your diplomatic status?'

'You don't need diplomatic status. These UN diplomats know hundreds of other diplomats. Diplomatic status may seem like a big deal back home, but once they get here it's only something that lets them park illegally without paying tickets. Most of them soon get blasé about their rank. But they never get tired of having fun. For many of them, UN duty means the most fun they've ever had. It's a super cure for homesickness. And their entertainment budgets! They get a terrific kick out of entertaining ordinary civilians like me. All you have to do is break into the party circuit and then it's the easiest thing in the world to spin from one delegation to another. You get to know people.'

'They must want to know who you are – what you are. What about security?'

'Security! That's a laugh,' Carmen said. 'I tell them I'm a spy. That always goes down well. They get good and tired of the public's general assumption that all diplomats are spies. Some UN delegates are just fun guys whose governments want them to take a long vacation from domestic politics. I'm not saying they're not serious fun guys. They're against World War Three and the man-eating shark. In the early stages, when I'm introducing myself, I usually hit them with the truth. I tell them I'm a graduate student. That's almost the whole truth. I sometimes attend lectures at the New School. I like the English seventeenth-century metaphysical poets. Who doesn't? It's a subject that gives me a lot of conversational leeway. I play it by ear. Let me show you.'

She consulted a book on her desk and picked up the telephone.

'Trinidad and Tobago?' she said. 'Please may I speak with the Ambassador? Dr Thorpe isn't in? She isn't? Oh, sure, it is early. How about the Chancellor? – er, Mr Wattley. Thanks. Hi, Lennox. Yes, isn't it? Like Port of Spain before a hurricane. It was a fun party with the Uruguayans, wasn't it? Look, I'll have a guest with me on the thirty-first. Is that OK? Patrick – ' She put a hand over the mouthpiece and got the rest of my name and passed it on. 'From Ireland.' She raised her eyebrows at me. 'Or England. He says he bowls off-breaks.' She lowered the telephone again and asked whether I bowled over or around the wicket. 'Yes,' she said into the telephone, 'that's what I always say. Good. See you.'

'Of course,' I said, when she had hung up. 'That was easy. He already knew you. But if you were starting from scratch . . .?'

'No problem. Suppose we – suppose I – wanted to go to the Belugastan thing next week. I'm not at all sure they're even members yet, but if not they're certainly here and doing their best to be lovable. Well, I'd phone them and say – all right; it's simpler to do it.'

Carmen called information and soon had someone who got someone else who spoke a language like Berlitz English.

'Good morning,' she said. 'This is Carmen Stott. I wish to speak with the Chief of Mission. Your leader. You are? First, may I congratulate you and the brave people of Belugastan on achieving your freedom while maintaining friendly relations with the Soviet Union and all other democracies. You're welcome. I have always admired the culture of . . . your region, and I wish to establish a close relationship with your delegation in order to improve the mutual understanding of our peoples. Yes, of course. In fact, I propose to organise a Friends of Belugastan Study Group here in New York. That's right. Perhaps it would be possible for me to become acquainted with you and your associates at next week's celebration of your independence. Thank you, that would be lovely.' She scribbled on a notepad. 'I look forward to that, Mr Zukolov. Ciao!'

She hung up and grinned.

'Like taking candy from a baby!' she said.

'You did that very well,' I told her.

'That's the formula for the easier ones. It doesn't always work, of course, but it does often enough. The bigger the nation, the more ingenious you have to be. The United States is the worst. The so-called Third World delegations are the most hospitable with the least red tape. The First World's OK after a couple of drinks. The whole universe is probably all right, once you get to know it.'

I thanked her warmly for the useful lesson. She gave me a Xerox copy of the list. We sat on wrought-iron chairs in the patio for a final cup of coffee. I felt silly now that I was wearing a dinner jacket in brightening sunshine. It seemed to be time to leave.

'There isn't a UN party tonight,' she said rather wistfully. 'But you wouldn't want one every night.'

As a token of my gratitude, I invited her to accompany me to Sardi's that evening. I had been keeping an eye on the Broadway companies of British musicals, and one of them fortunately was celebrating the end of a long, successful run.

'All we have to do is vaguely suggest Hollywood,' I assured her.

Although my fondness for steel bands is second to nobody's, I excused myself from the Trinidad and Tobago party that Friday. It is better not to get into the habit of tagging along with a partner, no matter how comely. It has been my experience that 'He freeloads best who freeloads alone.'

7

THAT August presented my first chance to penetrate the United Nations Organisation at home. I had visited UN personnel in Korea, Egypt and the Lebanon, and had found them to be sympathetically receptive. But those had been makeshift times when their recreational facilities and cuisine were not up to much.

In Korea, during what President Truman called the police action, one of the disappointing stalemates of Cold War realpolitik, the Danes were the jolliest hosts. Their contribution to the UN cause, characteristically, was a hospital ship, the *Jutlandia*, stationed off Inchon. The ship's white paint gleamed, and her brightwork glittered, as splendidly as a yacht's. The *smørrebrød* (like Swedish *smörgåsbord*) was good, then rivalled on that ill-catered-for peninsula only by the meals of the Ethiopians and Turks. The Danes are always profligate with schnapps, lager and merriment. But how long can one stay aboard any hospital ship, eating and drinking gargantuan quantities and playing jazz records, with a clear conscience, if one is in no need of medical attention? Alas, only a few days.

Now, dismounting from a Yellow Cab at One UN Plaza on a late-summer morning swept clear by a Force 3 breeze off the East River, I faced United Nations Headquarters. Was it my oyster? – my oyster Rockefeller? It was an inspiring prospect.

At first I stood and stared at the flags, flapping from a row of poles, like a military parade along the front of the complex. The flags are perfectly uniform in size: China, the Soviet Union, the United States and Sao Tomé and Principe have equal votes, at least in the General Assembly. There were very few flags that I could identify. It must be as difficult to design a new national flag as to compose an uplifting new national anthem. How many can you remember? Most flags and anthems are immediately forgettable, and possibly should be. The United Nations flag itself is admirably idealistic, with none of the hot blood-red of nationalism. The UN olive wreath embraces a map of the world in the light blue of heavenly clemency.

Looking across a neat strip of grass, I saw the dome on the low, curved roof of the General Assembly Building and, on its right, the thirty-nine-storey turquoise glass wall of the front of the Secretariat, a palace of bureaucracy, a mirror in which the outside world can see its anxiety and hope reflected.

The Secretariat, the Conference Building and most of the General Assembly Building are closed to the public, except on the frequent guided tours held daily but for New Year's Day and Christmas Day. I decided to go on a guided tour as a preliminary reconnaissance.

'There is all sorts of symbolism at the UN,' according to Miss B. Barrett, an official guide exuding the platonic allure of a perfect nurse in the svelte UN-blue uniform of a perfect air stewardess.

As the Security Council was not in session, Miss Barrett showed us the empty chamber. The Norwegians provided the handsome and encouraging décor. There was symbolism in the recurrent emblems in the blue and gold silk tapesty on the walls: 'Wheat for prosperity,' she explained, 'hearts for brotherhood and love, anchors for security.' And there was symbolism in the pictorial mural beyond the Council conference tables: 'The past is represented by conflict, the present by a phoenix arising from the ashes.' In the Trusteeship Council's empty meeting room, decorated by good old Denmark, a statue of a girl had her arms upraised, 'reaching out for the bluebird that symbolises happiness and freedom.'

The whole place was bright with promise. The acres of marble and carpet were immaculate. There didn't seem to be a single mote in the silently ventilated and conditioned air. My spirits remained buoyant even when we descended to the shops in the basement.

At the United Nations Postal Administration counter there was an array of special UN stamps, which may be used for mail posted in the building. One sales poster said that among philatelists 'discussion of the stamps inspires discussion of the United Nations itself.'

In the United Nations Bookshop, the books included *Controlled Thermonuclear Fission Research* and *Fun Around The World*.

The United Nations Souvenir Shop offered 'UN charms' (costume jewellery), cloth shoulder-patches embroidered with 'UN – We Believe', and a cookery book, *Favourite Recipes from the United Nations*. Then I noticed United Nations ashtrays, which were inscribed with the toasts of many nationalities, including 'Ram! Ram!' (India) and 'Good Luck!' (universal), and I was reminded that in London at that time the pubs were opening.

I thanked Miss Barrett for her delightful, informative guidance, which would be completed to my entire satisfaction if she would only let me know how to get to a United Nations bar. She smiled as though she thought I spoke in jest.

'Visitors are permitted to eat in the Delegates' Dining Room,' she said, 'but I'm afraid the Delegates' Lounge is closed to the public.'

This disclosure came as a nasty shock, but it was not one for which I had come unprepared.

The armed, uniformed security guard at the entrance to the Secretariat was a bulky, well-laundered man with a black moustache and aviator sunglasses. He extended a hand, palm uppermost. I suppressed a foolish impulse to put money into it.

'Good morning, sir,' he said. 'Your pass, please.'

I presented my letter of introduction on a sheet of the Prime Minister's writing paper. I should think there are many other sorts of paper that would serve. The text was brief and open to any interpretation that would satisfy the reader's requirements. It said:

THE PRIME MINISTER

To Whom It May Concern:

This is to introduce Mr. Patrick Skene Catling, of many years' experience of domestic and foreign affairs. He has established a special relationship with this office.

On a recent visit to Number 10 Downing Street he elected to pursue certain lines of confidential enquiry in order to validate assumptions of short- and long-term informational relevance.

Any courtesies you extend to him will be appreciated.

(signed)

The signature is one of my own, which in no way minimises the document's integrity, authenticity and effectiveness. Forgery is illegal and unnecessary.

The guard studied the piece of paper long enough to read the words two or three times. He slowly shook his head and clicked his tongue against his palate.

'Frankly, mister, you got me with this one,' he said. 'I'll have to get a ruling from Protocol and Liaison.' He picked up his telephone. 'Wait over there a minute, please.' With a gesture, he indicated how I could unblock the doorway.

Within ten minutes, a young man in seersucker came along. His hornrims and tidy little beard gave him the appearance of a conservative academic. He carefully scrutinised me and the paper and me again. While he submitted me to his steady gaze, as if trying to read my mind, I noticed him lightly fingering the embossed coat of arms at the head of the letter. The Braille tickle of fine engraving always makes a favourable impression on people who are easily impressed.

'Have you checked in with State?' he asked in a flat voice that an American Professor Higgins might have been able to place in the great plains. 'The State Department,' he added.

'I thought you yourself would have sufficient authority,' I wheedled flatteringly. 'But if you like – '

'Sure we have. What is the purpose of your visit?'

'I'm on a fact-finding mission,' I replied, using the Congressional euphemism for junketing. 'An in-depth feasability study. A hands-on interpersonal interface conjectural look-see. *You* know.' If you tell someone he knows something, a contradiction is very rare.

'Is there any specific requirement . . . ?'

'At first,' I said, 'I want to make myself known personally to some of the delegates, on a one-to-one basis. Cross-sectionally. I'd like to go in and . . . mingle. Face-to-face encounters are the best kind, don't you agree? I imagine that before lunch . . . the Delegates' Lounge might be the place?'

'Well, if that's all,' the P&L man said, looking relieved that apparently he wasn't going to have to do any work on my account. I gave him a sincere, underdone smile, to show how humbly undemanding and grateful and respectful I was. He waved the letter at the guard, and said: 'Gosh, this is good enough for me. We can issue you a temporary pass. Readily renewable. If you have any questions after you get the feel of the situation, you can give me a call in Room 201. If I'm not available, one of my colleagues will be able to advise you.'

'Thank you very much, Mr . . .'

'Kite. Bob Kite. Welcome to the UN. Have a good day now.'

I had an excellent day.

The United Nations Delegates' Lounge is a bar second to none. It really is worth making an effort to get into it. The room is pleasingly long and spacious, airy and light, with a lofty ceiling and stately windows. The sumptuously padded seats and the soft, pastel colours are in the very best tradition of contemporary international Good Taste, worthy of this year's newest Hilton. It is immediately obvious that one has entered an oasis for VIPs.

I caught a glimpse of the East River glittering in the sunshine before turning my attention to the bar itself, whose immense length and comprehensive shelves of bottles presented an exhilarating challenge.

Shortly before noon, there was already a lively crowd, mostly men, a few of them in the ornate, exotic costumes of high-ranking

Africans. I noticed a yellow man with a shaven skull in a monkish brown robe and three swarthy Brazilian colonels in dark green uniforms extravagantly beribboned. The majority wore light-weight dark suits that gave them the appearance of delegates to an international convention of senior businessmen.

There was a general enthusiastic babble of conversation. As I slowly strolled toward the far end of the bar, diligently eaves-dropping all the way, I passed many animated groups and heard several languages that were strange to me. However, the *lingua franca* evidently was English, in a rich variety of dialects.

There were several efficient, hard-working bartenders. Holders of the UN catering franchise must make a bundle. I was able to get a vodka and tonic with half a fresh lime and a merry tintinnabulation of ice cubes in a tall glass without any irksome delay. The price was gratifyingly low, and the drink was the last one I had to pay for. This was when I met His Excellency Sir Freddy Ngouamba of Laruba, an Old Etonian, a Balliol man, a barrister (Lincoln's Inn) and an eminent terrorist.

In late middle age, he had a paucity of grizzled curls like steel wool, but his figure was athletically trim (real tennis and polo). He was wearing a double-breasted navy-blue linen blazer with mother-of-pearl buttons, a Travellers Club tie, light grey Daks, white canvas shoes suitable for yachting, and a frown of woeful sombreness. He was standing alone with one elbow on the bar, looking down at a mint julep from which he seemed to be deriving little solace. I felt a pang of sympathetic understanding.

'It's not a bad day, though, for August,' I suggested.

He responded with a ghastly imitation of a smile.

'Do they make a good julep?' I asked, directing his mind to a possible cure for whatever malady was grieving him.

'The second one is usually of noticeable benefit. This is the first.'

'Let me get you the second,' I said. The offer was genuine, but I did not persist when he demurred.

'I'll do it,' he said in a manner which I recognised as authoritative. My sensitive expense-account detector registered 100. 'What's that? A G&T?'

'Vodka.'

The very word made him wince as if stung by a scorpion.

'That's what I started on last night,' he said. 'Then we went on to Jollies – '

71

'What's that?'

'The Delegates' Social Club. In the summer it's at Montauk, out on the Island. I thought everyone had heard about it by now. There have been so-called exposés. It's a sort of health club – a pool, Jacuzzi, sauna, massage et cetera. The et cetera have been the cause of all the scandalous rumours. After a week here at the UN, we have a right to let our hair down, so to speak.' He wryly scratched his scalp. 'Anyway, I didn't get the chopper back to town till mid-morning. I'm somewhat below the weather.' He ordered me a double and a large mint julep for himself.

Drinkers of industrial quantities usually get some sort of morose satisfaction from describing the symptoms of their hangovers. Sir Freddy was no exception. There was hypochondriacal talk of parrots' cages and pigsties, runaway metronomes and funereal church bells.

'But cheers anyway!' he concluded bravely.

Over his third drink, his mood perceptibly brightened. I spoke of life in Belgravia, Chelsea and Soho and we found that we had some acquaintances in common – the late Peter Alexander, for example, Merilyn Thorold, Christopher Moorsom, Muriel Belcher, all experts, in their different ways, on the art of high life.

'I always enjoy London,' Sir Freddy said. 'But I had to return to my homeland. The South Africans were enforcing the pass laws with swingeing severity. I organised an underground action group of freedom fighters – a bit of sabotage here and there. Not much more than pinpricks at first, but they had a cumulative effect. We were condemned as terrorists until the government needed someone to negotiate with and to unload our country on. Our part of South Africa was mined out and the soil was thin and poor. There were a few thousand square miles of useless land with a hungry, angry population, so the Afrikaners generously declared our independence. Laruba is a public relations creation. Not the most productive of republics, but our own.'

He ordered more drinks.

'I was our first Minister of Economics. That was when I first visited the United States, to come to Washington to beg for loans from the World Bank. I like American women and American music. I don't suppose you know the origin of our national flag. I chose the colours – black, brown and beige – after the title of a composition of Duke Ellington's. When Laruba joined the

UN and a few of us were offered the opportunity to serve in New York, I was ready. I imagine you wonder about my knighthood. That was my idea. I established our honours system, so that our ambassadors could get better tables in restaurants and better theatre tickets and so on. Like the citizens of most other democracies, Americans are very rank-conscious.'

Sir Freddy was definitely warming up. His black face was shining with recovery.

'Feeling a bit better?' I said.

'Infinitely. Thanks.'

'That last one did the trick.'

'Don't ever say anything about a last one.' He crooked a commanding forefinger at the nearest bartender. 'Now look who's come in. A large Chivas on the rocks, barman.'

The latecomer's creased red face and anxious yellow eyes betokened a wish that he had come earlier. He had shaggy grey hair that resembled cobwebs after a severe electrical storm and wore a dark grey summer suit of some drip-dry fabric which looked nothing like as miraculous as it had in the shop. Perhaps he had slept for several days in a transcontinental bus, or not slept.

'You must meet John Goodspeed,' Freddy said. 'A distinguished Texan. He's been with the Organisation almost since the beginning. Name an agency and he's done it – the ILO, FAO, WHO – '

'Very funny, Freddy. You're ahead of me.'

'John's got a nice racket these days,' Freddy told me. 'He's in WIPO. That's the World Intellectual Property Organisation. It's a specialised agency so special that nobody knows what it does, not even John.'

Before attempting to make a response, John silently took his glass and emptied it into his mouth.

'For your information,' he said with something that had to pass for dignity, 'I have left WIPO. I've switched to UNESCO.'

'A good move!' Freddy applauded. 'The United Nations Educational, Scientific and Cultural Organisation is much easier to hide in, and it has a big budget. You've latched onto something really esoteric, I bet.'

'You may mock,' John said, sliding his empty glass across the bar and significantly raising his eyebrows. The bartender complied. 'I think I have a very interesting little project in the works.'

'Do tell us about it, if that wouldn't be a breach of security.'

'I am having Dylan Thomas's classic radio play *Under Milk Wood* translated into Slovene and recorded in Yugoslavia.'

'Something that had to be done,' Freddy said, nodding in approval.

'Then I'm taking the tape on a tour of Polynesia. There'll be a lot of intercultural feedback.'

'And it'll get you out of New York and into the South Pacific in time for Christmas,' Freddy pointed out.

John swivelled his glare in my direction.

'You're not saying much. What do *you* do?' he demanded.

'I'm just visiting. Part of an open-ended investigation of the big picture.'

'But which agency is subsidising you?'

'None of them. I'm not operating under the UN umbrella. I'm an independent.'

'Are you free for lunch?' Freddy asked. 'I think maybe I have an idea for you, if you're not too busy. You'd better come with us, John. You can catch up at the table.'

'I'm not eating in that Delegates' dining room,' John protested. 'The last time I ate there the room was full of tourists.'

'We're not eating there either,' Freddy said. 'I once had lunch there and the cocktail of the day contained grappa and grenadine. We're going to P. J. Clarke's. I need a transplant of extra-rare hamburger.'

So we went to Third Avenue and played Irish songs on the jukebox. Then we went on to a number of other places. Somewhere along the line, John said he had to go to discuss a reading of Paraguayan sonnets with a girl in Tuckahoe. Freddy and I continued. We tried without much success to sing with Bobby Short. We managed a hot rice dish in a café run by Vietnamese boat people in Spanish Harlem. It wasn't till we ended up at Gregory's, on East Ninety-something, or possibly East Sixty-something, at about two o'clock the next morning (there was a new cornet player who growled like the late Wild Bill Davison), that Freddy got around to telling me what he had in mind.

Naturally I said yes.

8

ACCOUNTANTS in Kraalville, the capital of the Democratic People's Republic of Laruba, are very much like accountants in Milton Keynes, Buckinghamshire, and Toledo, Ohio.

Each of them lives in a small mortgaged house in a new development of identical small mortgaged houses. He has a wife and 2.2 children and is considering the advantages of a vasectomy. She has an inexorable ambition to own conspicuously more consumer durables and consumer perishables than the neighbours and maintains an encyclopaedic knowledge of up-market advertisements and feature articles recommending the latest improvements in something of will-o'-the-wisp unattainability called Lifestyle. The children have the appetites of vacuum cleaners, grow out of their shoes with speed worthy of the *Guinness Book of Freaks*, and require state-of-the-art electronic means of communication with the pop scene.

The typical accountant commutes early five mornings a week to an office in a downtown no-parking zone in a car slightly bigger than the one he drove last year. This one has electric self-cleaning ashtrays, though he doesn't smoke. He still owes the bank almost two-thirds of the cost, plus interest in double figures, which will increase immediately after the next election.

Punctually at 1 pm he eats a low-cholesterol sandwich, constructed of dark bread supposed to ward off constipation, and drinks a slimline citrus cola, at his desk. He notices that most of the executives go out for two-hour lunch hours and return laughing and exuding gusts of peppermint. Even the office boys go out for lunch in the nearby pubs. They live with their parents and are able to keep their wages in their pockets for whimsical disbursement.

When the accountant has to process expense accounts, often for luxurious indulgence authorised by the beneficiaries' pals, he suffers an acute acid pain below the heart and an almost irresistible urge to scream. Usually, however, if he cannot detect any procedural or arithmetical irregularity, he grits his teeth and passes the reluctantly initialed paper into his out tray. And feels that he has died a little.

Accountants can be dangerous to your corporate health. In the advanced stages of jealousy and paranoia, they make increasingly determined efforts to subvert fellow employees, particularly those who venture into the field, where life would be unbearably lonely and austere with insufficient funds. The most malevolent accountants of all are those who become civil servants, putting the brakes on expenditure of tax monies, which they come to believe should be conserved in a niggardly hoard, as if it were their own.

I quickly surmised that what Sir Freddy Ngouamba had in mind was what every playboy-diplomat often has in mind, ie, the thought that the music may suddenly stop and there may be no chair to sit on. In spite of Freddy's privileged ancestry (for many generations, his family owned vast herds of cattle, in the days before Dutch brucellosis), in spite of his costly education, his charm and his friends in high places, he was prey to the fears which make the hour between 4 and 5 am the most terrible of the twenty-four.

'I've been doing a rethink about your proposal, Freddy,' I said when we met in the Delegates' Lounge at midday, as arranged, for tequila therapy. 'I appreciate your confidence in me after such a short acquaintance, but – '

'Please, but me no buts,' he interrupted, somewhat agitatedly. His central nervous system apparently had not as yet quite knitted together; his central cortex was obviously nagging. There is nothing more depressing than a bullying superego when one is not feeling absolutely up to the mark. It was likely that he was also experiencing twinges of peripheral neuritis in the big toes.

'As I said last night,' I said, 'I'd like to go. A trip to Laruba would not seriously disrupt my schedule. I can understand your hesitation to – '

'Not only hesitation. I can't go myself. My calendar is chock-full of commitments. Libya tonight; Viet Nam tomorrow; Qatar on the third, and Swaziland on the sixth. September's the biggest month. I couldn't miss Mexico.'

'I suppose it's possible that I could do you some good that you couldn't very well do for yourself. An apparently unsolicited testimonial from me could perhaps be helpful. If you really are anxious about your status *vis-à-vis* the Finance Minister. Too bad he went to Harrow. And then, as you pointed out, there's the President to consider. Even presidents unfortunately can be influenced detrimentally by the money men. And – '

'And my wife,' Freddy groaned. 'I have a wife there. She insists that we need a larger pool. The whole government's getting larger pools.' I had not known about the wife in Kraalville. The lady in New York to whom he had referred in a jocular but affectionate fashion late in our tour of nightclubs was evidently a mere surrogate.

'Well, I could have a word with Lady Ngouamba, if you like,' I conceded. 'I could tell her how hard things are in New York. The climate. The hours. The cost of living. But are you quite sure it wouldn't be better if you took some leave and went back to see them all? No?'

He shook his head vehemently.

'No. You. I want you to go. I'll make it worth your while.'

'I require no honorarium,' I said. 'I'd be glad to do you a favour. Besides, I'm interested in developing countries. In the dynamic phase, there's so much one can do in them, isn't there?'

'You're a man of the world,' Freddy said. 'Tourism is going to be our main source of revenue, apart from the International Monetary Fund. You could give the Minister of Tourism a few tips. He's not too bright, but he's an old friend and a jolly good host. We once shared a girl in Burford. I'm sure he'll show you a good time. He'll lay everything on. Everything. If you need a plane to get around in, just say the word.'

'All right, Freddy. I'll do it, for you. But please don't expect me to stay more than a few weeks. I have to be back in London by the end of September.' He agreed to my stringent conditions.

'I'll send a Fax to my Ministry of Foreign Affairs,' he promised, 'telling them all about you.'

I must have looked startled.

'All you decide they need to know,' he added placatingly. 'You can write it yourself while we're having lunch. I thought we might go over to the Brussels. They do a nice gigot, and I'm sure you'll approve of the cellar. We'll also fax your letter. That letter'll wow 'em. We're all madly Anglophilic. The President almost graduated from Dartmouth. He cruises around Lake Laruba in a souped-up trimaran dressed as a bloody admiral. We're actually pro-almost-anything as long as it isn't Afrikaner.'

I'd forgotten showing him my Number 10 to-whom-it-may-concern letter, but obviously it had not done any harm. It had been a very long evening. Late in a long evening is a good time to embellish one's identity.

My only regret was that I'd miss the Mexican party. I didn't blame Freddy for not wanting to miss it. I'd been looking forward to that one. I'm a marimba aficionado.

As if he had detected a niggling doubt, Freddy quickly got us a couple of tequila sours and said: 'It'll be easy for you to convince the Cabinet how essential my work is here at the UN. I know you can do it with a few well chosen words. You'll be very comfortable at the Grand Kraal Hotel. You'll have a chauffeur-driven limo, and anything else you want. You'll like Larubair. For the next few weeks of touristic conferences, we're chartering Concorde, and we've got some marvellous steward-esses. We'll fix those accountants!'

Among the many advantages of flying in a British Airways Concorde from London to New York or Washington is that in the Concorde departure lounge at Heathrow passengers are permitted to make free telephone calls to numbers anywhere in the world. The only catch is that shortly before 11 am London time it is difficult to think of any friends in America who would welcome a call. Very few people are at their chattiest when awakened by the telephone at dawn. No matter how heartily one laughs while telling them about the excellence of the buck's fizz, the responses, more often than not, are negative.

The first time I flew across the Atlantic at no cost to myself was during World War Two, not long after I began shaving every day. I was a navigator in 45 Group, RAF, a mixture of Air Force and civilian aircrew of various nationalities, whose job was to ferry aircraft built in Canada (Lancasters and Mosquitoes) and the United States (Baltimores, Marauders and Dakotas) to Britain, North Africa and India.

In time for Christmas, 1943, I was posted to Nassau, the

western terminal of the RAF's ferry route across the South Atlantic. Some RAF doctor, to whom I shall always be grateful, had decided that we should undertake no more than one delivery a month to Egypt or India, so we often found ourselves with two weeks a month resting in the Royal Victoria Hotel and boating and swimming off Paradise Beach.

The comfortable, private accommodation and excellent meals were free, of course, and I never felt hard-pressed financially. Like other aircrew of the South Atlantic Wing, I was doing a nice little trade in Angostura bitters, rum, Brazilian Swiss wristwatches and imitation Chanel 5, at a mark-up of 2–3,000 per cent east of Suez. How innocent compared with modern smuggling! Some of us (I understand) were augmenting service pay by purchasing five-pound notes for three pounds each in Cairo. The Germans were forging the fivers and distributing them in the vain hope of causing a loss of faith in sterling currency; however, the faster money circulated in the Middle East, the better everyone felt about it. The forgeries were of such high quality that the Bank of England had introduced banknotes containing strips of metal. They must have been difficult to implant and were meant to baffle imitators.

Returning from ferry flights as passengers with A-1 priorities in British and American military aircraft, we usually travelled across North Africa and thence back to Nassau via the Azores, Bermuda and Miami. RAF clerks typed our travel orders on ordinary Mimeograph paper. I could type as well as they could, so I prepared special orders for my pilot, radio operator and me, directing the air force despatchers of the free world to route us according to the vagaries of the seasons and our own moods. For example, I once typed that 'This crew is to be returned to base by way of New York', and so that was the way a C-54 Skymaster of the obliging USAF took us. I elected to make the northerly detour in order to see the original Broadway production of *Oklahoma*; the USO was giving servicemen free tickets.

Similarly, on the long journeys eastwards (flying from Nassau to Karachi took about ten days, in short hops), I used to vary our routes, sometimes choosing to land at offbeat aerodromes, where we could be sure that bored station commanders would give us a warm welcome to the mess, and the civilian women in local towns had not been sated by the company of men in uniform.

But enough of war.

As Concorde took off from JFK that September morning, flying under the auspices of Larubair en route to Accra, Ghana, and Kraalville, I remembered my first Concorde flight nearly ten years earlier. The memory of the thrill remains ineradicably imprinted. Even the most travel-jaded diplomats, tycoons and pop stars get a kick out of this most elegant machine.

The captain of my first Concorde allowed passengers, one by one, to visit the flight deck. I marvelled at all the gadgets, especially the Machmeter, which indicated that we were flying at 1,340 mph, and the altimeter, which read 58,000 feet – faster than a rifle bullet, at twice the height of Mount Everest, as advertised. The Glen L. Martin Baltimore, a twin-engined bomber, when encumbered with a belly-tank for long distances, used to cruise at about 220 mph at 9,000 feet.

Awed by technical progress, I went back to my seat and tried to regain a sense of proportion and arouse a sense of new adventure by reading James Michie's vigorous translation of the odes of Horace. Sipping Hine VSOP, I soon came across some apposite lines (Book Three, Ode 25):

> *Bacchus, where am I? Flushed*
> *With god, to what groves, caves, am I being rushed*
> *Inspired?*

and

> *... Welcome the sweet delight*
> *Of danger! Lord of Wine,*
> *Lead on! I follow, crowned with your green vine.*

Now, happy to be aboard Concorde again, I rethought of those brave Horatian sentiments as I drank dry sherry and relished the prospect of roast pheasant supplied by Larubair.

Good old Laruba! Good old Freddy! Good old UN! Good old Carmen! As Louis Armstrong so rightly observed, 'It's a Wonderful World.'

9

C ONCORDE flew straight in, touching down on time with the most discreet of squawks. There was no other traffic in the air and only one other plane on the ground, a Jumbo 747 bearing the colours of Larubair, parked in front of a hangar. One of its engines was being stripped by men in overalls, perhaps accounting for the need to charter the plane I had arrived in. There were many acres of new-looking tarmac where nothing was happening. Across the white façade of the control tower and passenger and freight terminal building, there was a sign in letters about ten feet high: WELCOME TO KRAALVILLE INTER-NATIONAL AIRPORT.

As in so many other countries which have experienced a period of membership of the British Empire and Commonwealth of Nations, the Customs and Immigration inspectors and airport police were dressed in uniforms of British military design, tan bush jackets with brass buttons, long shorts, and Guards' caps with those smart vertical peaks which almost completely obscure the wearer's eyes.

Approaching the first counter, I produced a passport, but an African in a white pith helmet and a white linen suit hurriedly intervened, waving my document back into my pocket. It was the Minister of Tourism, the Rt Hon Sir Winston Otuba, MP, himself. Freddy must have prepared him well. He couldn't have been more cordial.

'There's no need for any formalities,' Sir Winston assured me, 'except, of course, to say that we are delighted to receive you as an honoured guest of the Republic.'

The few other passengers were less fortunate. They were having their clothing unpacked and strewn about hither and thither, jars of cosmetics probed, tubes of shaving cream and toothpaste severely squeezed, and bottles of shampoo

84

and perfume emptied, in a thorough check for contraband.

Sir Winston ushered me out of the customs hall and away from its wails and groans. A porter followed me with my suitcase and Concorde dark blue flight bag, which, it must be emphasised, should always be taken as a high-prestige status indicator whenever one travels, whichever the airline, train or bus. One can undoubtedly obtain Concorde bags and Concorde tie-on labels without having to fly Concorde.

Although nobody had inspected me, it was now my compulsory privilege to inspect a guard of honour. This élite unit had transcended colonial traditions: they wore the splendid plumed golden shakoes and gold-frogged scarlet tunics, pale blue jodhpurs and purple patent-leather riding boots, golden spurs and golden gauntlets of some camp couturier's Ruritanian operatic wet dream. While they presented arms with chrome-plated Czechoslovakian machine-pistols, a small military band whomped and squealed and thudded the Laruban national anthem, – 'Excelsior, Laruba!' – which had been so recently composed (in New York's Brill Building), and so little rehearsed, that the tuba and glockenspiel found themselves at cross-purposes time-signaturewise.

Anyway, it was the thought that counted. I was moved. I wondered what next.

Conditioned by novels and films, I had expected vultures perched on the rusty tin roofs of unpainted wooden shacks, innumerable naked children, goats and chickens, dusty dirt roads and flamboyant weeds. And that, in fact, was what I saw, but only blurred in the middle distance. The black Mercedes stretch limousine, with a black-brown-and-beige pennant fluttering from its left front wing and dark green anti-glare, anti-peeking-in windows, rushed us at high speed along the two miles of ruler-straight, six-lane concrete autobahn from the airport to the Grand Kraal Hotel.

Sir Winston gave my elbow a chummy squeeze.

'We thought you'd probably like an hour to yourself, to have a shower and change and rest after your journey,' he said. 'There'll be a reception for you at the Presidential Palace at six o'clock. Ah, here's the hotel manager, Sir Xerox Tsokanwa. He'll fix you up. Xerox, here's our VIP.'

Sir Winston gave me a sort of salute, flourishing the conjoined tips of the thumb and forefinger of his right hand to signify that everything was under control. So it was.

The soft carpeting, the conditioned air, the Muzak *Aspects of Love* in the lift and in my enormous suite, The Midas Suite, which overlooked the swimming pool, tennis courts and pitch-and-putt golf course, made me feel as away-from-home as if I had come to Singapore, Marbella or Torquay. On a table beside my fawn silken king-size bed, a telephone was winking its red eye to tell me I had already received a telephone call.

It was Freddy.

'How are you getting on?' he asked. I could tell that he was making a serious attempt to sound jaunty. I also realised that he was attempting the impossible: it was still too early for him to have availed himself of the healing powers of the Delegates' Lounge.

'I just checked into the hotel,' I replied.

'Is your room all right?'

'Fantastic. I'm in The Midas Suite. It's vast.'

'I know. It incorporates some of the amenities of The Oliver Messel Suite at the Dorchester, including a hidden bar. See the bookcase against the wall opposite the windows?'

I did.

'Those aren't real books – only the leather bindings of real books. Like the Dorchester, we've put the key to the booze in the spine of a biography of St Francis of Assisi.' Freddy managed a feeble chuckle, which seemed entirely adequate.

'You didn't call to tell me that, did you?'

'All right,' he said. 'There's no need to get ratty. When are you meeting Sir Max? Maximilian Ngomo. The PM.'

'At six. An hour from now.'

'Good. Here's what I want you to tell him. I don't like putting this sort of thing in writing. Say I'm confident I can swing the loan from Chase, if he increases my entertainment allowance by another fifty grand. He'll know what entertainment means in this context. Ha, ha. That's his personal loan I'm talking about. The money for the casino is already in the bag. He'll be able to return the funds that were borrowed from the hydroelectric dam project. OK?'

'I suppose there's no danger that this phone is bugged?'

Freddy's laughter sounded a bit heartier.

'We're not that efficient,' he said. 'I had you booked into the Marie Antoinette Suite and changed at the last minute. A joker in the overalls of a telephone engineer will be coming to see you later, no doubt.'

There was a buzz at the door. Freddy was right. He had called just in time. I told the man with the bug to come again when I'd be out.

'That's all I wanted to say,' Freddy concluded. 'After you've passed on that message and told Max how wonderful I am, you can concentrate on having a good time.'

I said I'd do my best, but I was already feeling a bit uneasy. I try never to get too *involved*.

The limo and its liveried chauffeur were waiting in front of the hotel at 5.50. We arrived at the Presidential Palace, a large, Italianate pink villa that would have fitted harmoniously into Beverly Hills, at precisely 5.59. At 6.00 the Minister of Tourism presented me to the Prime Minister and I had Sir Max's beautifully manicured chubby right hand in mine.

The reception was held in the ballroom. On the bandstand at the far end of the room, illuminated by a chandelier but half-concealed by potted palms, a string quartet in white ties and tails played Mozart behind twenty simultaneous loud conversations.

After the exchanges of pleasantries about Concorde and the awful August climate of New York, the Prime Minister led the way to an adjacent, small drawing room, where we were able to sit in comfort, while he picked the part of my brains that I offered for picking. He seemed pleased by the message from Freddy.

'Sir Freddy speaks highly of you,' Sir Max said. 'The next time you see him, say I think it's about time to have another go at the World Bank. It's not the sort of suggestion I like to put in writing, you understand, and phones are so leaky these days.'

I nodded noncommitally, as I had no immediate intention of returning to New York.

'Money's such a bore, isn't it?' Sir Max said with a deep sigh, speaking, he must have thought, as one financier to another. 'We can never rest from fund-raising.

'We were considering hiring a first-magnitude Irish pop star – Irish is so neutral – to organise a spontaneous concert, with a worldwide satellite TV link, to collect money for Laruba Famine Relief. We would have been willing to distribute a percentage of the proceeds to our rural population in the form of dehydrated porridge. Some of it would have been bound to get through.

'We were thinking of getting Reuters and the Associated Press to send out some starvation pictures,' he went on, 'but my cousin Billy, who has the Laruba State Tourist Board offices in New York, London and Tokyo, said media projection of nationwide famine in Laruba might tarnish our image. Apparently most foreign tourists wouldn't like the idea of spending a holiday among a lot of kids with sad faces and swollen bellies and skinny little arms and legs. Apparently foreigners prefer to have their recreation where it doesn't make them feel guilty. We've decided not to publicise our famine areas, which we are keeping well clear of our safari park and multisports stadium.

'We are now contemplating the possibility of holding a Madonnathon in the stadium. Madonna is a young lady with whom foreign tourists would like to relate. She has earned many platinum discs; and, of course, her very name is a plus.'

I merely kept nodding. By the end of his monologue, the Prime Minister was well satisfied with me as an expert adviser. With honeyed phrases, he returned me to Sir Winston for circulation among the other guests, who were members of the government, diplomatic and business community and their wives and companions.

A few glasses of sweet sparkling Burgundy later (South African wines are not proscribed in Laruban government circles), a clock chimed authoritatively seven times, and most of the guests, without having to be told, paid their final respects and got lost. The Minister of Tourism a little later bade farewell to our host and conducted the remaining, favoured guests, including me, to a cavalcade of half a dozen limousines.

The next stop proved to be a long one, at the El Dorado Race Course and Country Club. We dined lengthily (terrapin, octopus, wild boar and jelly doughnuts au flaming rhum) on a private terrace above the clubhouse.

While we sat at our tables, stewards in red blazers ran in relays to the pari-mutuel tellers below, to place our bets on the greyhound races. Races were held every fifteen minutes throughout the evening under floodlights. Sir Winston's tips on the dogs were absolutely infallible. By the end of the last race my pockets were bulging with high-denomination banknotes. Laruban dollars were said to be of some value in the government gift shop, open only to senior officials and holders of temporary cards.

Sitting out a dance in the Country Club nightclub, I was approached by a distinguished-looking silver-haired white man with a French Legion of Honour rosette in the buttonhole of his dinner jacket. He introduced himself as the American ambassador to Kraalville.

'I hear you're from the UN,' he said.

'Well, yes, *from* it,' I agreed punctiliously.

'I imagine you sometimes run into Sir Freddy Ngouamba.'

'Yes, I do sometimes.'

'Great guy, great guy!'

'Yes, isn't he?'

'Hmmm. Look, the next time you see him . . .'

'Yes?'

'I wonder whether you'd do me a favour?'

'Of course. If I can.'

'Please don't mention that you met me in this . . . place. With the lady I'm with. I mean . . . to tell you the truth . . . frankly . . . but . . . my wife in Scarsdale, you know . . . Enough said?'

'Quite enough,' I said, with a friendly wink.

Less than half an hour later, the British ambassador took me aside and went through a similar palaver. Freddy was a friend of his too. In fact, Freddy had pulled some strings to get him his post in Laruba. He'd appreciate my discretion the next time I was at Number 10.

'I gather that you and the Foreign Office people are pretty thick, what?' he suggested anxiously.

'Oh, I wouldn't say *thick*,' I said, implying thickish.

'I'd be awfully grateful if you'd keep this evening . . . under your hat, so to speak. My partner for the evening is only the friend of a friend. He had to pop over to the UK, you know.'

'I didn't even know you were here,' I said.

'No, quite. But one can't be too careful. I thought I'd just mention . . . people in London might get the wrong end of the stick.'

'My lips will be sealed as far as you're concerned.'

'I say, thanks awfully, old boy.'

What did these people take me for? Some sort of possible blackmailer?

And then I wondered: was there a possibility that I might find myself a blackmailee? I thought the atmosphere was rather strange.

By two o'clock in the morning, I was becoming sleepy. Even Concorde causes some jet lag, if you fly far enough.

When I opened the door of The Midas Suite, I was ill-prepared for my welcome there.

Two exceptionally pretty, nubile young women, a brown one and a pale-pink one, were sitting side by side against a heap of silken cushions on my king-size bed. They wore orchids in their hair. Their clothing was negligently gossamer.

I eventually felt I had to tell them that they should leave, unless they had nowhere else to spend what was left of the night.

When I went down for lunch, I thought about the extraordinary chain of events that had resulted from my having attended a lecture on Wells Cathedral at the English-Speaking Union. Wishing not to push my luck, I decided not to stay too many more days and nights in Laruba.

As a newly reinstated bachelor, I was living at one time for a nominal rent, about half a peppercorn, in the basement of a friend's house in Wilton Place. The address was superior to the accommodation, a hastily improvised flat, a bedsitting room with a record player and a dim back room in which the functions of a kitchen and a bathroom confusingly overlapped.

Wilton Place was close to The Star, which, in the late Paddy Kennedy's day, used to be the Belgravian headquarters for certifiable villains, and closer to The Grenadier, which was crowded on weekends with debs and pseudodebs and their delights, and even closer still, through my landlord's garden and a few yards along the mews, to the Nag's Head.

The Nag's Head was said to be London's smallest pub, and Len must have been London's fattest publican. He was a most amiable man. He appreciated music. He had a Victorian music box, which played large brass discs perforated like Pianola rolls. There was also a Victorian musical device on the bar, a brass birdcage containing on a perch a moth-eaten grey-yellow mechanical canary. An old penny in a slot caused the canary to chirrup for a couple of minutes. No matter how oppressively cloudy the day, the birdsong created a hopeful illusion at least that the sun might shine. When the currency was decimalised to appease Eurobankers and make arithmetic easier for British schoolchildren, the Nag's Head retained an old penny for recycling through the birdcage as long as there were clients who cared.

Len had a shrewish little wife who might well have given the pub its name. She nagged him incessantly until one day, without any warning, she died. The effect on the widower, who had been devoted to her all along, was pitifully immediate. He shrank, like a punctured balloon. He made me realise that when alone one must take strenuous efforts to amuse oneself, to get out and about.

An RAF friend, in semiretirement at a desk in Whitehall, kindly arranged to let me fly at no expense in a spare seat aboard a British United Airways plane chartered for Joint Service Air Trooping, enabling me to spend a long weekend in Hong Kong.

'This'll be better than Singers, eh?' suggested a Navy lieutenant in the next seat. 'Haven't been to Singers recently. Not much good now. Can't trust the Malays. Honkers much better. Lots of fun and games. Antismuggling patrol. Can't really stop it, of course. Thousands of small junks moving about at night. But still. Good training for a job outside later on, eh? – I mean running some millionaire's yacht on the Riviera or something like that.'

The last time I had visited Hong Kong, I had taken a side trip in the *Lee Hong* ferry to Macao and met Michael Patrick O'Brien, alias Robert Stephens, alias Stephen Stanley Ragan, a stateless vagrant who had boarded the vessel at Macao three hundred trips before. Now neither Hong Kong nor Macao would let him go ashore again. He looked like Humphrey Bogart in *The African Queen* before Katherine Hepburn's influence made him clean-shaven.

In the *Lee Hong*'s noisome saloon, while we chugged westwards past Lantau Island, he told me the story of his life in reformatories, jails and military stockades, of hold-ups in the United States and some trouble with a knife in a nightclub in Shanghai. When he produced a bottle of No. 1 Scotch Whisky: Guaranteed First Class Edinburgh Grapes, I soon recognised that keeping him aboard for ever would be a violation of the human rights which Eleanor Roosevelt had done so much to codify for the United Nations. I therefore composed a letter to the International Court of Justice, and he signed it in the persona of O'Brien. It isn't always certain which are a chameleon's true colours. Anyway, some months later I read in *The New York Times*, or possibly *The National Enquirer*, that he had been accepted by the Dominican Republic, where I imagine he felt right at home.

Hong Kong this time was more built up, more congested and more frantic than ever. I wondered what the place would be like when it became part of China in 1997.

In the China Products Company department store in Kowloon, a shop which is supposed to be a showcase for the craftsmanship of the Chinese People's Republic, I squandered nearly a pound on a *yee woo*, an onomatopoeically named two-stringed violin with a wooden dragon's-head handle. It didn't seem worth that much, especially when I read a sign on the noticeboard of the Hong Kong Club shortly afterwards saying that no musical instrument should be played on the club premises without the General Committee's consent. There was no chance of obtaining that, but otherwise the old hands of Butterfield & Swire and the rest of them were generously hospitable. Perhaps I was rewarded for not playing my *yee woo*. I briefly considered the advantage of always carrying one not to play.

The tailor whose sweatshop made me a sharkskin suit overnight was one of the colony's countless tailors who claim that their patrons include Eddie Murphy and the Duke of Edinburgh. The suit was a bargain, or seemed to be until the first time I had it cleaned. It turned mauve.

My best buy on my hit-and-run weekend visit was a box of incense candles from a souvenir shop on the waterfront near the Luk Kwok Hotel, which is known locally as the Suzie Wong Hotel. My attention was seduced by a sign in the shop window: 'Mandarin Candles – The Artistic Novelties of Our Handicraft Production Most Lately – on Special Occasion When These Candles Are Lighted It Would No Doubt Add Some More Happy & Delicate Atmosphere to A Social Party.'

The Wilton Place basement needed all the happiness and delicacy I could muster.

Electric and Musical Industries added temporarily to the happiness if not the delicacy of my life in the basement by issuing a series of HMV records of sound effects. They made a welcome change, at first, from the chunky, slightly sour piano solos of Thelonious Monk, who was beginning to make me feel too sad. The sound effects were dramatic intimations of a world of action. The emphasis was on mechanical disturbances and disasters, which made solitary confinement underground seem cosy.

'Car Effects' typically included 'approach and stop, door slam; door slam and depart; reverse, with horn; horns, sirens, approach and skid; crash.' 'Air Liner' quickly deteriorated from 'passing overhead' to 'engine noise or roar, nose-dive, crash and fire.' 'Trains' came to a terrible end with 'express crash' and the hiss of steam from a ruptured boiler. Turned up to play as loud as actuality, the records gave immense pleasure to my landlord's six-year-old son in an upper room. There was one record of the highest fidelity that had an unexpected effect.

One fine Saturday afternoon, St Paul's Church, on the other side of Wilton Place, was gathering a smart throng for the third wedding ceremony of the day. The guests, in formal attire, were strolling about in the forecourt in the deliberately casual manner in which fashionable racegoers parade in the paddock at Royal Ascot.

When I played 'Air Raid on London', loud and clear, with my windows wide open, the effect of the warbling siren was dynamic. Led by the more elderly guests, the congregation hurried into the church at the convulsive tempo of Keystone Cops. The record proceeded with appalling realism past 'planes approach, AA gunfire, bombs fall' and had reached the jangling clangour of 'fire engines' when there was heavy knocking on the door.

Fortunately, I resisted the temptation to play 'Dogs' ('house dogs barking, Alsatian barking, Alsatian howling, small dogs barking, yelping, barking at distance, terriers barking at intruder'), and the policeman, who had hurried over from church duty, was really very nice about the whole thing.

'I was bored,' I explained.

'Maybe,' he gently reproached me, 'but a wedding's a big event for the people concerned. You could've given someone a heart attack.'

My remorse was almost genuine, and the good officer let me off with a caution.

I had forgotten that most couples getting married for the first time like the idea. I remembered weddings I had enjoyed, wedding receptions ... Wedding receptions! I suddenly saw how foolish I had been, allowing recent events to blind me to past pleasures. Though wishing for social diversions, I had neglected to apply to St Paul's, a most conveniently situated medium of gratis luxury.

During the following week and the week after, I studied the Social News in the *Daily Telegraph* every morning, as assiduously as a horseplayer scans the form in *Sporting Life*. St Paul's does a brisk business in fashionable weddings, so my patience was rewarded. There, below Court and Social, among the paid announcements of Forthcoming Marriages, was what I was looking for:

> *M Marcel Autrechose and Venetia, Lady ffrith-Ponsonby*
> *The marriage will take place at St Paul's Church, Wilton Place, on June 4 between Marcel, the eldest son of the late M and Mme Jean Autrechose, of Chamonix-Mont-Blanc, and Venetia, Lady ffrith-Ponsonby, second daughter of the late Lord and Lady ffrith-Ponsonby, of Nether Pining-in-Marsh, Gloucestershire.*

A telephone call to the church ascertained that the ceremony was scheduled to take place at 11 am and that morning dress would be in order.

Having removed the previous evening's frying pan and plates and glasses from the tub, I had a bath which I prolonged by occasionally nudging the hot-water tap with a foot, until my palms and soles were white and wrinkled. After an exquisitely close shave, I succeeded in finding a fresh pair of Jockey shorts, hanging with a string of Belgian onions from a hook beside the kitchen sink. My morning suit was immaculate, in the dry-cleaner's giant condom. I had decided to wear the suit with the hound's-tooth trousers, with the added decoration of a yellow silk waistcoat embroidered with tiny Pegasuses of many pastel colours, on the theory, which I have thoroughly tested, that if one's costume is ostentatious enough nobody suspects one of trying to hide anything. My gardenia *boutonnière*, on the other hand, was disarmingly modest.

Having arrived at the church early, before the ushers, I seated myself in a pew two-thirds of the way back, on the side of the groom, who, being French, seemed more likely than the bride to need support.

No such nice consideration was necessary, however; both sides of the aisle were well filled by eleven o'clock. The bigger the crowd, of course, the better, from the interloper's point of view. The intensity of scrutiny on such occasions is inversely proportional to the number of persons present. By the time the organ thundered the newlyweds out, I felt quite secure.

Outside the church, I chose a large, antique, dark blue Daimler cabriolet with a massive, leather-strapped touring trunk and an *F* for France. Sometimes a language barrier can serve as a protective fortification, and I am unable to speak French until late in the evening.

'A lift to the reception?' I asked the aristocratic-looking elderly couple who, with the chauffeur, had the spacious car to themselves. I pointed to myself and to them. 'Please may I accompany you? I have not brought my own vehicle.' As a matter of fact, I did not own one.

The man gestured towards one of the two folding seats in the shaggily carpeted, dove-grey rear compartment, which was as sumptuous as a pre-Revolutionary boudoir.

'Sure,' he said. 'Jump in.'

I did so, grinning somewhat sheepishly. Having made sure his passengers were comfortably arranged, the chauffeur shut the door and we set off. I wondered where the reception was going to be, and hoped that it wasn't in some remote Gloucestershire manor house. A few minutes later, I was relieved when we stopped in front of the Hyde Park Hotel. Free parties seem less free if they subsequently require taxis and trains. I vowed not to go to any more wedding receptions without finding out beforehand where they were to be held.

The Hyde Park is a good hotel. I have enjoyed staying there, always in one of the rooms at the back, looking over the trees and grass, away from the hustle and bustle of Knightsbridge. Now I was glad that I had abstained from breakfast.

I accompanied the friendly Daimler couple to the reception room. A man in the scarlet of a toastmaster with the mien of a sergeant major stood at the open glass double doors and alarmed me for an instant by asking me for my invitation.

'I'm afraid I haven't got one with me,' I admitted. 'I've just flown in from Hong Kong.'

I was counting on the fact that if one speaks fairly rapidly and yet in a relaxed manner, a non sequitur can sound like an explanatory sequitur. Plus the fact that there was a rather long queue building up behind me.

'This is supposed to be by invitation only,' the man said.

'We're together,' said the Daimler man, handing over the invitation for himself and his lady.

97

'We've come from the church,' I said, as if doubting my right of entry might be tantamount to sacrilege.

'Very well, sir. I'm only following orders. Come in.'

I thanked Mr Daimler, perhaps too profusely.

'That's OK,' he said. 'I used to do it myself.'

Once I was in, of course, there was no problem.

My perfunctory research in *Burke's Peerage* and *Debrett's* had been unnecessary. I needn't have spent any time consulting the Michelin guide or those old copies of *The Tatler*. Hardly anyone I encountered seemed to know anyone else very well, if at all.

'Have you come over from Chamonix?' a young woman ventured. 'I saw you sitting on the groom's side.' So my waistcoat had made an impression.

'Not just now. Actually, I've just flown in from Hong Kong.'

'Oh.'

'It must be lovely in Chamonix at this time of the year,' I added, willing to please. 'The garden of the Albert the First and Milan. *Jardin fleuri*'. So convenient for the Mont Blanc Tunnel. You're from Chamonix, are you?'

'I live in Maida Vale.'

Willy-nilly, in spite of my efforts not to be, I was introduced to the groom.

'Too bad Monsieur Autrechose couldn't have been here today,' I said.

'Did you know my father?'

'We're of the same generation,' I said.

'He hated society.'

There was a slight longueur.

Then Marcel's face brightened.

'Have you driven the new Honda Civic?' he asked. '*C'est formidable.*'

I could cope with that.

'In what way?'

'Ah! By increasing the rigidity of the piston skirt and using a very thin piston wall, a lightweight piston configuration able to realise high output power has been achieved.'

'That sounds good. By the way, these crab things are delicious.'

'They make Venetia sick,' Marcel said.

'What a pity.'

'Everything makes her sick. She's pregnant.'

The conversation at the reception was like the conversation at any ordinary London dinner party. The champagne was so-so.

I made another vow, which I have never broken. Although up-market weddings offer one great scope and may be worth attending in cases of extreme desperation, I vowed that I would avoid them in future, even if I ran out of baked beans.

I prefer not to dwell upon failures in a world where so many successes are attainable, but I thought it would be unfair not to warn you.

11

THE denizens of Soho are goldfish pretending to be piranhas. As the freeloading centre of the world, it is chock-a-block with pastmasters. The habitués of the pubs and clubs try hard to seem cynical and ruthless, but they are romantics with hearts of marzipan. They are warily defensive against people like themselves and quick to scent the fresh blood of innocents, but rarely suck all of it.

Daniel Farson, the most perceptive contemporary chronicler and photographer of the place, has observed: 'Soho has always attracted eccentrics rather than criminals.' In this era of nuclear weapons and nerve gas, can it be a crime to bum a drink?

It is against the policy of Ian Board, the Queen of the Colony Room, to buy drinks for members and their guests. But like the late Muriel Belcher, who founded the club and all its unwritten rules, in the tradition of the late Rosa Lewis of the Cavendish Hotel in Jermyn Street, Ian is very good at compelling people with ample funds to maintain a steady flow of drinks for everyone else. I cannot recall that he ever gave me a drink directly, but during the past thirty years or so there have been times when he has been the prime mover who initiated favourable impulses in others.

In Soho, every appeal for help is fairly considered on its merits, and the response is often sympathetic – if the appeal has been made honestly on grounds of sincere unworthiness. Prompt assistance is usually forthcoming, even for strangers, for whiskies and taxis, but hardly ever for coffees and bus fares. The motto is 'Waste, Want Not.'

The British Museum sells nice Christmas cards, so early in December I was staying in a hotel in Bloomsbury for my annual card-purchasing splurge. The late-breakfast scrambled eggs from

102

the steam table were lukewarm and the coffee was muddy and I wished I were elsewhere.

Looking through *Variety*, the definitive 'International Entertainment Weekly,' I read a news item that struck sparks. The paper is too big and important to kid around with Runyonesque showbiz slang in its headlines, as it used to, but it is still without equal as a reporter of the latest facts of the trade.

Jan Sizzars, the actress, feminist philosopher and entrepreneuse of the chain of martial arts studios that bear her name, was due to arrive from Los Angeles to promote the new sequel to *Karate Nun. Karate Nun III* had been almost as socko at the box office as *Karate Nun II*. Billie da Silva, the producer, said she was satisfied they had perfected the formula, she was very enthused with the mathematics, and predicted that *Karate Nun IV* was going to prove the biggest blockbuster in the beloved misandrist's boffola series. 'We're thinking powerful,' Ms da Silva was quoted as saying. 'This Christmas week should be the biggest yet.' I was thinking eureka.

I arrived at the Coach & Horses, Norman Balon's notorious refreshment parlour at the corner of Greek Street and Romilly Street, Soho, at 11.20 am precisely. I was sure that Jeffrey Bernard would be well into his second large vodka and soda and prepared to converse in a reasonably unsavage way.

As Jeffrey has been telling readers of his 'Low Life' column in *The Spectator* for many years, after his first two public drinks of the morning he usually feels less ghastly than before them. He has been seriously flirting with ghastliness for a long time, as a diabetic horse-player who had incurred involuntary celibacy through anaesthesia.

After three decades of sometimes severe financial vicissitudes in Soho, with only infrequent excursions to Barbados, Kenya and Thailand (freebies, need one say?), Jeffrey achieved national fame in depth and a certain deserved percentage of good fortune when Keith Waterhouse, an ace survivor of Fleet Street, scored a smash hit with a wonderful tragi-comic play, *Jeffrey Bernard Is Unwell*. It is based on Jeffrey's tumultuous life and astonishingly honest columns. The title is the sentence the editor of *The Spectator* has had to use occasionally to excuse unscheduled non-appearances of 'Low Life'. Peter O'Toole (inspired casting) starred in the play with triumphant success, and Tom Conti eventually replaced him, also to good effect.

As the play continued to pack the Apollo Theatre, there seemed to be a danger that discordant happiness might disturb Jeffrey's writing. Boyish smiles with increasing frequency were brightening his hard-earned facial furrows. But his habits and style are engrained deeply enough to resist change. When newspaper and magazine writers and radio and television crews came around to his pub for interviews, he allowed them to buy him large vodkas. Fans turned up and were not discriminated against. There was enough thirst to accommodate all of them.

Jeffrey and I have been friends for unmeasured years. By unmeasured, I mean neither of us had kept count of the money. If a tally had been kept, I believe it would be decently balanced. He is not a person of whom I find it difficult to ask a favour, especially on a morning like the one in question, which had started well for him, with Earl Grey tea and Mozart and no inexplicable pains.

'I was wondering whether you'd do me a favour,' I said, when drinks had come, clinking with the promise of a leprechaun's gold.

'I wonder why people say that before they ask,' he commented. 'Bloody twerpish really. Oh, well.'

I was glad to find him in such a good mood. If he hadn't been, his answer would have been shorter.

'You're planning to go to the Groucho later, I suppose, aren't you, for your nap?'

'I suppose so. Would you mind getting to the point?'

'All right. I need a sort of straight man. Not your usual rôle, I know. I want you to say a few antifeminist things to me, quite loud, in the Groucho bar.'

'Is that all? That's not a big favour. I'll get the next drink, after all.'

We got to the Groucho Club before two o'clock. The tables near the bar were occupied by the sort of high-powered publishing amazons I had been counting on. There was no sign of Michael Sissons, the literary agent, a member of the Club Committee, who might have cramped my style. He hasn't been able to take me seriously since he saw me bowled for a duck at Broad-Halfpenny Down, the historic cricket ground in Hampshire.

I was pleased to see Jessica Garnish of Medusa Press, Ilse Koch of Harridan House, and Bella Smidgeon, the new editor-in-chief of Jade Books. Perfect. Seeing them there, knocking back the spritzers and flourishing their slim black cheroots, I thought of the original Medusa, one of the three Gorgons, whose head, with writhing snakes for hair, turned all men who beheld it to stone, except for their private parts, which were turned to jelly. The women were talking excitedly and laughing a lot, as if discussing the men they were planning to ban from their next autumn lists.

'Talking of women,' Jeffrey said from his place a couple of yards from mine at the bar, 'talking of women,' he repeated, raising the volume, to make sure he had caught their attention, 'can you tell me why it is that some of them are actually allowed to decide which books are to be published and which ones are to be sent back to the wretched male hacks starving in bloody garrets?'

The opening gambit, which we had composed on the way over from the Coach, was obviously effective. The three women immediately stopped talking and regarded him with the penetrating intensity of laser beams.

'The reason is simple, Jeff,' I replied in the calm, thoughtful, persuasive voice of a soap-powder scientist in a television commercial. 'Women are simply better editors and publishers. Tests prove they have more acumen, more flair, more acuity, more of everything that editors need to be great, innovative, creative editors. Haven't you noticed the imaginative virtuosity, the dedicated commitment, the passion and eloquence of new novels conceived, written, edited and published by women? Where are the new Huxleys and Orwells, Jeff? There aren't any. The sacred flame of fiction is being borne forward by Penelope Lively and Margaret Drabble.'

'I think I know more about women than you do,' Jeffrey said. We knew that women don't like men to claim they know about them. 'By the end of the first year your average woman is reluctant to iron a shirt or boil an egg. Women editors have bad breath.'

'Women are the makers, Jeff,' I persisted, glancing quickly at Medusa, Harridan and Jade and wondering which of them would come through. 'Women make things happen. God is a woman.

She first created Eve. Adam was an afterthought, a joke made of surplus buttock. As soon as the genetic engineers figure out immaculate conception, we'll be out of a job.'

After a few more equally weighty exchanges, Jeffrey shrugged and disappeared for his customary siesta. I had to wait only a couple of minutes before Jessica Garnish sent word inviting me to join them for a drink at their table.

When Garnish and Koch retired, presumably for a routine secret conference in the loo, I grabbed my chance. According to *Celebrities Service*, the subscription newsletter that tells one where stars are staying, Jan Sizzars was due to check into the Savoy the following day.

'With your co-operation, Ms Smidgeon,' I said, 'I think I can get Jan Sizzars to sign with Jade. There's no time to waste. There's one detail I have to settle with you first. Perhaps we could go somewhere private.'

'You can call me Bella,' said Jade's new editor-in-chief, leaving money on the table and heading for the exit.

It was that easy.

12

RELATIVELY few good-looking teenage female groupies gain the attention they crave from macho young pop stars. After a very short time, the oily-haired, pimply musicians toss the girls away like used Kleenex. Grown men who wait with bunches of roses outside stage doors at night in the rain, or outside the doors of television studios, are still more pathetic. They are not even used as disposable sex toys. They are exceptionally lucky if their vigil is rewarded with as much as a scribbled autograph. Actresses and singers are usually hurried to their limousines by apelike bodyguards, who shoulder admirers aside as if adoration were a loathsome disease.

However, I have yet to hear of an ordinary megastar whose door will not swing open readily to anyone bearing a contract for her (or his) biography. From Bella Smidgeon, I had procured such a contract. It provided an immediate advance in six figures. That had been my idea, on the understanding that I simultaneously handed over to Jade Books my own cheque for an equal amount. Thus Ms Smidgeon was enabled to imagine she was making a coup, perhaps unprecedented in feminist publishing history. And thus I had the impressive credentials I required, without any obligation whatsoever. I promised Ms Smidgeon only that I was going to do what I could, and I certainly was.

Oh, yes; I know: there may be carpers who will complain that this arrangement amounted to misrepresentation on my part. My defence is that Jan Sizzars had profited enormously by misrepresenting herself as an actress, and Ms Smidgeon was misrepresenting herself as a publisher. I was striking a small blow in what James Thurber presciently described as 'The War Between Men And Women'. For the record, I would like to make it perfectly clear at this moment in time that I am not in the least tiny little bit opposed to women, as such; I oppose only those who oppose me. Sizzars had publicly declared herself to be an enemy of all men. Her whole career in movies and the martial arts was founded on misandry, her hatred of men. Ditto Jade Books. Hating men has become a major industry. They both accepted me with alacrity only because they took me to be a traitor to my unpopular gender.

I had been out to Hollywood more than once before, so I was not unready for lying and cheating. The first time I had gone there with a Mickey Mouse contract for a biography that I subsequently did not write was away back in the sweet-scented days when heterosexuality was a proclivity that dared speak its name.

Please don't say a word against Howard Hughes in my presence. Why shouldn't he have worn old tennis shoes? It was none other than he who paid for my visit, or wrote it off like his non-flying giant flying boat. He owned so much and was so rich and so absent from the scene that he was the ideal patron.

Howard Hughes owned Trans World Airlines, so I flew to The Coast in a TWA Constellation. You know that shot in many films which lingeringly shows an identifiable airliner in fine weather, because the production company owes the airline a plug in exchange for free transportation? If my biography of Jane Russell had been written, my book would have contained full-page photographs of a Constellation and the RKO Radio Pictures studios in Los Angeles, as well as Jane herself. In one way or another, Hughes then owned all three. He had the actress under a twenty-year contract. This excessive enslavement was an example of the studio system at its worst. It may account for the fact that when she was compelled to perform in absurd rubbish with a nonactor such as Victor Mature she appeared not to try very hard. During the same period, Hughes had Robert Mitchum tied up on the same terms – $2,000 a week, which was a lot at the beginning, but not much by the time he escaped. Mitchum was equally unenthusiastic about most of his RKO parts and demonstrated his reluctance on the screen with exhibitions of defiant apathy. Off the lot they were both a lot of laughs.

The studio system at its best was RKO providing me with a villa at the Garden of Allah, whose bar was animated by the benign ghosts of F. Scott Fitzgerald, Robert Benchley and Dorothy Parker, giving it the atmosphere of an Algonquin West. In the person of Perry Lieber, a publicist who didn't really give a damn how much RKO money I spent, the studio also provided a car (I chose a pistachio-green convertible with red seats) and apparently unlimited pocket money.

In the late 1920s, when Sunset Boulevard became rural only a short distance from downtown Hollywood, a Russian ballerina in exile had built the house which became the Garden of Allah's main building; the swimming pool was the shape of the Black Sea. My villa consisted of a bedroom and bathroom, a drawing room with a dining alcove, and a kitchen. The kitchen was useful for the manufacture of ice cubes.

Having read *What Makes Sammy Run*, by Budd Schulberg, *The Day of The Locust*, by Nathanael West (my favourite downbeat Hollywood novel) and Evelyn Waugh's *The Loved One*, I was prepared to despise everything I found there; but, I admit, I was enchanted. All the minor walk-on characters must have come straight from Central Casting.

'How do you like your martini?' enquired Rocky, the Garden of Allah bartender, who looked like a superannuated middleweight who should have retired earlier, yet whose manner was as unctuously urbane as Jeeves's.

'Dry.'

'Very dry?'

'Very dry.'

He poured Beefeater with a strong, steady hand into a large, wide-open champagne glass and murmured over it, softly, just once: 'Martini and Rossi.'

At midmorning, breakfasting in dappled shade on the terrace by the pool, I saw a dwarf in a big Mexican straw sombrero and a tiny bikini, lying on his belly on the warm tiles, reading *The Hollywood Reporter*, while a big blonde in sunglasses, bikini and high-heeled yellow shoes leaned over him and fondly anointed his muscular shoulders with sun lotion. He was resting between his weekly performances as a teddy bear in a live TV commercial for orange juice. 'He does it very well,' a waiter testified.

There was still something of an English colony in Hollywood, including the kindly knight in a monocle whom Waugh accurately caricatured, an old man with an old friend, sitting outside a bungalow with whiskies by a 'dry water hole' (an empty swimming pool) at sunset, 'the counterparts of numberless fellow countrymen exiled in the barbarous regions of the world.'

I visited a set where Mitchum was impersonating a US Army colonel with a minimum of zest.

As he was the star of the picture, he had a comfortably furnished trailer as a private dressing room in the hangarlike studio.

When I arrived, at about 8.30 in the morning, he was eating sardines and overripe Limburger cheese, which smelled like sweaty socks. A beaker of amber fluid was fuming sweetly on a hotplate.

'Have some *sake*,' he suggested.

Perhaps I held my nose.

'I'm scheduled to make love this morning,' he said disgustedly. 'If there's anything I hate it's making love on an empty stomach.'

He also particularly hated being obliged to simulate making love to Jennifer Jones, an actress who attempted to compensate for a lack of talent with almost suffocating gentility. She had not as yet overcome the reverence she had felt for herself as Saint Bernadette.

The third time an assistant director nervously requested his attendance at the big love scene, Mitchum slowly ambled over to his co-star and heavily aspirated at her.

'Hi, Jennifer. How's tricks? Have we-all gotta start kissin'?'

The wave of putrid cheese and warm Japanese rice wine made her flinch, but she got through the scene somehow.

'You've almost got to admire the woman for that,' he commented grudgingly, as we returned to his trailer.

'This trailer smells like the burning ghats of the Ganges,' he said. To his secretary, he said: 'When you're in Beverly Hills, get some incense, for God's sake.'

'Incense,' she acknowledged.

'Make it jasmine.'

'Right. There's Scotch in the cupboard and plenty of ice.'

'The girl's a genius,' he said to me. 'Now how did she know that I want to get good and *dronk*.' Bad scripts often had that effect on him.

111

We drank a bit, agreeing that Chivas Regal is better than *sake*, for ordinary everyday use.

'Pour another,' he said. 'I wrote a book once, a novel. I don't know what happened to it. Before that I drove trucks. Writing, driving, acting – what's the difference? I'll tell you one thing: playing colonel out there is the easiest way I know to get the dough to pay for Scotch like this. It's twenty years old, man.'

Mitchum's day's work was over. Mine wasn't even going to begin.

That night we went to hear Joe Bushkin play piano at a Hollywood jazz joint called, appropriately, The Hangover. Joe and we stayed after the place closed, not long before dawn. By then all three of us were drinking brandy and white crème de menthe – aptly named stingers – out of highball glasses.

When Mitchum grabbed the sizeable bill, I said: 'Let me get that,' and he did.

'I pay, you pay; who cares? It isn't real money – it's Howard's money.'

A couple of hours after we left the nightclub, the sun rose and Mitchum had to return to the studio. He said he'd shower and shave in the trailer.

'I think I'll stay with brandy this morning,' he said, donning the uniform with the silver eagles. 'I don't think Jennifer likes *sake*.'

Those were some of my best days in Hollywood. Perhaps you can imagine the worst ones, such as when Michael Caine provided abundant white wine in his hilltop eyrie but no lunch, and when I told Peggy Lee's butler I wished he wouldn't keep the claret in the refrigerator.

13

I N spite of her proud, upright stance and svelte muscles, Jan Sizzars turned out to be a pushover. Though it was a trifling sum compared with the multimillion-dollar deals to which she was accustomed, my £275,000 advance convinced her that Jade Books respected her philosophy.

'I'll instruct my agent to take care of you when you get to Beverly Hills,' she promised. 'Here's her office number. I'll see you at the end of next week.'

By happy chance, *Harpers & Queen* that month had named 'the 50 most beautiful women in Britain: not actresses, not models, but people you might share a taxi with.' One of them was Charlotte, my youngest daughter. The magazine documented its entirely reasonable accolade with a full-page portrait of her by Angus McBean, a photographer whose sensitive and dramatic use of light and shade I immediately learned to admire.

The advantage of being one of the fifty most beautiful women in Britain would be hard to measure. Among the spin-offs that affected me right away as next of kin was that someone gave Charlotte two return tickets from London to New York, and she generously invited me to accompany her on the flight.

'It's on Kuwait Airways,' she said.

'That must be all right,' I replied. 'Kuwait's one of the richest countries in the world. Their planes must be sound.'

At Heathrow (yet again), she bought me a drink and left me for a few minutes. She had not criticised the tie I was wearing, but on her return she gave me an elegantly subfusc paisley silk tie, dull burgundy, chocolate brown and dark green, by Paco Rabanne of Paris. She did not actually urge me to put it on right away, but of course I did.

The plane was shiny and comfortable and had the proper

number of engines and I looked forward to the journey with hardly any fear.

There was one disappointment. When we levelled off at 38,000 feet and we were allowed to unfasten our seat belts, I was pleased to see the drinks trolley coming down the aisle. When it reached us, however, the stewardess, who must have been one of the fifty most beautiful women in Kuwait, asked whether we would prefer orange or Coca Cola. Even when I disclosed that I was not a Muslim, she was unable to offer anything else to boost my morale for the rest of the way.

We arrived in New York without any further difficulty. Quite thirsty though. When we reached the Algonquin, I was delighted to find Andrew Anspach in the lobby. I had known him for many years as the hotel's excellent managing director. Many a time, he had indulged me by seating me at Table 26 in the Oak Room, the legendary Round Table; he had introduced me to Ella Fitzgerald in the Blue Bar; he had always guided me to the most interesting new shows in Broadway theatres; and knowing of my curiosity about food at all stages of preparation, he had sent me to meet Gerry Stack, formerly of County Kerry, at the Fulton Fish Market at five o'clock one morning, an experience whose memory I treasure. Gerry had warmed the grey dawn by pouring Paddy into the coffee. The market warmed the cockles of the heart with a poster which said: 'Make a Cow Happy – Eat a Fish.'

Sitting in the lobby, which was the same as I remembered but brighter, because it had recently been entirely redecorated, Andrew ordered drinks for the three of us before telling me some shattering news. A Japanese company had bought the hotel. He was no longer the managing director, but was being retained as a consultant. He smiled as bravely as the Spartan youth with the hidden fox gnawing his vitals.

'Let's have another drink,' Andrew said.

About an hour later, Charlotte and I left the hotel. Rain was falling. The doorman's whistle failed to summon a taxi. We walked to Fifth Avenue. The rain was falling harder and all the taxis were occupied. Standing on a corner beside a traffic light, we were beginning to feel damp. This was another time I had a good reason to appreciate her beauty.

One of those enormous yellow garbage trucks hissed and grunted to a halt beside us as the light turned red.

Charlotte smiled up at the driver, a great Sonny Liston figure in blue overalls.

'Hello!' Charlotte said, delighted to see him. 'Could you possibly give us a lift?'

'Come *on!*' he replied with an incandescent white grin.

She climbed up the steep metal steps and I followed.

'Thanks a lot,' Charlotte fervently gasped, reflecting his smile with a pretty terrific one of her own.

'Where to, lady?'

'We're trying to get to the 21 Club.'

The lights changed and the truck lurched forward with a roar.

'Twenty-one!' the driver shouted.

Maybe it wasn't out of his way to drive us a few blocks up Fifth Avenue. But then he swung around to take us right to the doors of the club.

Towering above the black Cadillacs and Rolls-Royces which always line the sidewalk there, the yellow truck attracted a lot of attention. Chauffeurs in their black peaked caps and uniforms applauded as Charlotte stepped down. I expected the painted metal statuettes of jockeys at the entrance to cheer.

Compared with a garbage truck, the limousines seemed so commonplace.

I was not surprised that word of her exploit reached the maître d' and that he arranged to serve us a drink on the house.

For some women freeloading is very, very easy. But then it isn't regarded as freeloading.

I was grateful, of course, but my suite at the Beverly Hills Hotel, the silver-grey Porsche and the meals at Ma Maison, though gratifying, were rather tamely anticlimatic.

14

C ULTURE is sometimes the key to the horn of plenty.

Santa Fé, New Mexico, the oldest state capital in the United States (established in 1610), was full of tourists. There was an arts fair in the plaza – silver and turquoise jewellery and acrylics of Indians leaning against adobe walls. I decided to move on to Taos, a smaller, even more remote, comparably ancient town about seventy miles farther north.

As I had no car and there would not be a bus for several hours, I asked a policeman in the street whether the authorities objected to hitchiking. He was one of the new style, young, academic policemen. He had probably composed Zen haikus.

'I have no objection to *your* hitchhiking, if that's what you mean,' he answered pedantically. '*I* wouldn't do it. But it's your life.'

I was travelling light, carrying only a few essential personal effects in my Concorde bag. I walked along Route 84 about a mile beyond the outskirts of town, to show that I was sincerely trying to get somewhere, and started waving my thumb.

An open lorry stopped. The back was fully laden with *piñon* logs, the resinous local firewood. I sat beside the driver. He had long black hair and dark brown eyes and a complexion like beige leather. He wore blue denims and cowboy boots. He spoke only Spanish.

'You're Mexican?' I said. In New Mexico there isn't much point in mentioning that the weather once again is perfect.

'Hispanic-American,' he corrected me.

That nicety of racial nomenclature having been clarified, we got on quite well, well enough for him to pass me a realistic black plastic replica of a telephone, and to show me how to unscrew one end of the imitation receiver, so that I could drink bourbon whiskey from it. But just when the journey was going fast and smoothly, he suddenly veered off the highway on to a narrow dirt road and pulled up.

'This is my turn-off,' he said. 'Goodbye. Good luck.'

I needed it, I realised; when I returned to the highway I found myself in the middle of one of those long, straight stretches of which there are so many in that open part of the country. The few cars were whizzing by at high speed.

In a region renowned for its blue skies, the weather became uncharacteristically threatening. The sun was westering behind ominously dark clouds over the Rio Grande Valley and sheet lightning was flickering silently among darker clouds accumulating over the Sangre de Cristo Mountains. I was reminded of the understatement of Chesterton's *Noah*: 'It looks like rain, I think.' I imagined being marooned, soaked, miles from the nearest habitation, as darkness was about to fall.

But then there was a sudden squeal of tyres, and a small, pale blue Chevrolet slithered to a halt beside me and the door opened.

The driver was Lesley McDougall Brown, an energetic and fortunately impulsive widow in her seventies, daughter of the late William McDougall, a distinguished psychologist. After teaching at Oxford and Harvard, he had concluded his career as head of the psychology department at Duke University, in Durham, North Carolina, where he encouraged Dr J. B. Rhine to found its celebrated and controversial Parapsychology Laboratory.

Professor McDougall, according to one of his publishers (he was a prolific author), 'developed the concept that all behaviour is purposive and directed towards a goal.' Every inch her father's daughter, Mrs Brown recognised that I was not standing beside the road without a reason. Perhaps some inherited interest in psychopathology made her want to find out what the reason was. Perhaps in some old-fashioned way she was simply kind.

Having spent most of her adult years in America, Mrs Brown was a skilful interrogator of strangers. Americans do not hesitate to probe the heart of the matter, the who, what, where, when, how and why of things. Somehow, we engaged in a conversation about poetry and painting. It became apparent that she herself was a sometimes poet and that she still painted bright, impressionistic watercolours of distant mountains under big skies.

'Like long-distance Dufy?' I suggested.

We learned that we had both met W. H. Auden at university cocktail parties after poetry readings and had not really liked him an awful lot. The insistent short a's of his late New York period had seemed false. Maybe he felt he owed them to his hosts.

The cultural and social life of Taos is dominated by painters and people who talk about painting. In a population of three thousand or so there are perhaps a hundred painters who support themselves by selling their work in the thirty-nine local galleries. Most of the buyers are summer tourists and winter skiers. But, though painting is the principal artistic activity, the presiding genius of the place is D. H. Lawrence, one of the great freeloaders of the twentieth century.

'Mabel Dodge Luhan,' Mrs Brown said as we drove along, 'a wealthy American patroness of the arts who married her Indian chauffeur, invited Lawrence and Frieda, his wife, to come here. Mabel *insisted*. That's the sort of person she was.' And that was the sort of person Lawrence was; he always succeeded in making his benefactors insist.

'She gave the Lawrences the Kiowa Ranch, on the side of Mount Lobo. They visited Taos only briefly, really. But Taos was the only place in America that Lawrence ever considered home. They lived here intermittently from 1922 to 1925, with trips in between to Mexico and England. In London, Lawrence managed to persuade Dorothy Brett, the daughter of Lord Esher, to come to live with them on the ranch.' Lawrence was willing to share what he was given. 'That didn't last long. Frieda – very jealous – threw her out. But Dorothy stayed here for the rest of her life. She was a good friend of mine. I have some of her paintings.'

As we drove beside the Rio Grande, Mrs Brown told me of Lawrence's final journey back to New Mexico.

'Lawrence died in Vence, in the South of France, in 1930, and he was buried there. Frieda married an Italian, Angelo Ravagli, but she still cared enough for Lawrence to build a shrine in his memory near the ranch house. And in 1935 she sent her husband to Vence to disinter Lawrence's remains, cremate them, and bring the ashes back to the ranch. When she met Angie at the railroad station at Lamy, New Mexico, there was some confusion. The urn containing the ashes was left on the platform. Frieda and Angie had driven twenty miles before she noticed they'd forgotten Lorenzo and they had to go back.

'Then,' Mrs Brown went on, 'there was some wrangling between Mabel Luhan and Frieda. Mabel said the ashes didn't belong to Frieda; they belonged to the world. Mabel said she, Mabel, ought to build a bigger and better shrine. Dorothy warned Frieda that Mabel planned to kidnap the ashes, so Frieda rather cleverly made sure they couldn't be taken away. She quickly buried the ashes in concrete in the altar of the shrine at the ranch. Some people say she actually mixed the ashes with the concrete. Lawrence was securely immured.

'When Frieda died, Angie buried her just outside the shrine. In her will she left the ranch to the University of New Mexico. The university awards an annual Lawrence fellowship to a writer who wants to spend a few months working where Lawrence wrote so much.' Thus freebies beget freebies.

By the time we reached Taos Mrs Brown had divulged that she was leaving very soon for a two-month vacation in New England and the West Indies, and she had offered to appoint me custodian of her house while she was away.

The pretty adobe house, with Dorothy Brett paintings in the master bedroom, is situated at the dead end of a quiet cul-de-sac at the rear entrance to Kit Carson Cemetery, where the nineteenth-century trapper, scout, army officer and Indian agent lies buried. Across the gravestones there is a splendid view of the sacred mountain of the Taos Indians. The boundary of the tribe's 90,000-acre reservation is only five minutes' walk from the house, and Taos Pueblo, the strictly protected Indian village, is only three miles inside the reservation.

The day after I settled temporarily in Taos, I drove Mrs Brown's Chevrolet to the plaza. Walking across the central garden, I was pleasantly surprised to encounter an acquaintance from London, Kenneth Bradshaw, who was clerk of the House of Commons. He brought me no news of mutual friends and Parliamentary politics. All he could talk about was D. H. Lawrence.

'You've seen the Lawrence paintings, I suppose,' he said. 'You haven't? There they are, across the street, in La Fonda Hotel. I've

121

spent a very interesting hour with the owner. Saki Karavas, his name is. Charming man. Well, I must be getting on. I have to drive over to see the Lawrence ranch.'

Saki Karavas, a Greek-American, bought ten of Lawrence's oil paintings from Frieda and kept them in the small office of his hotel. They were ten of the thirteen paintings which the Home Office ordered seized from the Warren Gallery in London in 1929 on the grounds that they were obscene. In the event, the police agreed not to destroy the paintings on condition that Lawrence took them abroad and promised never to try to take them back to England. It is difficult now to imagine what all the fuss was about. The mystical eroticism of Lawrence's fiction became on canvas an unruly tumble of boneless flab. His roly-poly nudes look as though he had made them of Plasticine. Rebecca West made the best comment on them.

'Mr Lawrence,' she wrote, 'has very pink friends.'

Mr Karavas showed me a dossier of letters from people who wanted him to give them the paintings. He did not intend to give them away. There was a typical expression of his sentiments in a reply to a request from the Humanities Research Center of the University of Texas.

'Should there not be sufficient interest in the purchase of the paintings,' he wrote, 'I intend to leave them to Greece. Since England has the Elgin Marbles, I thought it only fitting that Greece should have the D. H. Lawrence paintings.'

I told Mr Karavas that I did not expect him to give the paintings to me. I did not put any undue stress on the word 'give' to imply that I was thinking of possibly buying them. But he took me to lunch anyway. We went to a restaurant on the other side of the plaza. The grilled swordfish steak and Chablis was quite all right.

Greer Garson, the retired film actress, who was living on the Forked Lightning Ranch, at Pecos, New Mexico, presided over a D. H. Lawrence Festival on the fiftieth anniversary of his death. There was a fancy-dress ball at the Mabel Dodge Luhan house in Taos, for which the guests dressed up as characters in Lawrence novels. Naturally, there were many rival Lady Chatterleys and gamekeepers. A special punch was concocted for the evening, containing, among other ingredients, a high proportion of anisette and a creamy Italian almond liqueur. The deadly mixture was called 'The Plumed Serpent'.

IF one hangs about in the proximity of the rich some of their affluence is likely to rub off. Imaginary or reflected affluence, creatively projected, can be like the real thing. One doesn't have to do much. In fact, the less one is seen to do, the better. Activity may be considered rather vulgar, like noticeably striving to succeed.

One September weekend, for want of anything better to do, I was dining thoughtfully on oysters and grouse at a window table in the rooftop grill of the Hôtel de Paris in Monaco. Before leaving London, I had sent myself a telex at the hotel (469925), informing me that Coutts, 'as instructed', were arranging the transfer of 354,000 francs (an odd amount is always best) to my bank in Lyon. More than once, I have thought I would like to have an account there. It would be less obvious than Paris, and where can one eat better than with Paul Bocuse?

The Hôtel de Paris does not judge its clients merely by financial standards, but there isn't any hotel where evidence of super-solvency does any harm. The manager of the Hôtel de Paris was warmly welcoming. It's a good hotel. I did not plan to stay long, so I took a pleasant, sunny room with a southerly view over the port.

A friend at the Victoria Sporting Club in London, which, from its inception, was always noted for practicality rather than high social gloss, had confided that the Taj Vegas Hotel had an agent in Monte Carlo that weekend and had given me a Polaroid snapshot of him. Cy Perino, as he was calling himself at the time, resembled Jackie Gleason in his famous rôle of Minnesota Fats, the pool shark – well fed and as nattily tailored as a bent tax attorney. Perino was on one of his regular tours of the costlier European gambling resorts, in his employers' never-ending crusade to lure high rollers to the hotel casino.

124

There was a period when I occasionally used to be disturbed on the telephone at three or four in the morning by the manic, conspiratorial calls of Randolph Churchill. On an earlier visit to the Hôtel de Paris, I had felt obliged to pay my respects to Sir Winston Churchill as he stood in the lobby, holding the usual unlighted big cigar, awaiting the arrival of the private lift which Aristotle Onassis had had installed for him. Onassis was a collector of celebrities even before he met Maria Callas, and Churchill enjoyed being the frequent guest of one of the richest ship- and yacht-owners in the world; the two men were made for each other.

Sir Winston gruffly acknowledged that Randolph was indeed his son. Onassis, to whom I then introduced myself, had a remarkably retentive memory. Several years later, when by chance we were seated on adjacent banquettes upstairs at 21, where I was reluctantly lunching Ginger Rogers, he put down his hamburger long enough to say, 'Hey, Pat! What the hell you doing over here?'

Now, on this latest expedition to Monte Carlo, when I saw both Onassis and Cy Perino in the hotel lobby before lunch, I made a point of going over to Onassis for a ritualistic big hello and one of those prolonged double handshakes that gangsters esteem as proofs of deep friendship and that you are not holding a knife. I was sure that Perino was observing us.

Arriving at the Grand Casino early that evening, I stood between a roulette table and the entrance to the *Salon Privé*, where the bigger baccarat players are permitted to win or lose fortunes. When I saw Perino come in, I walked slowly away from the *Salon* door, as if I had just been in that room of hazardous great opportunity.

Perino cordially addressed me by name.

'I don't believe we have met,' I murmured in a slightly pained voice *privé*.

He handed me a large, gilt-edged visiting card, which identified him as a vice president of the Taj Vegas Hotel & Casino Corporation. He then invited me for a drink, which I agreed to accept.

'You a friend of Onassis, right?' he said.

'Ari? Oh, we've known each other for some years.'

'You a player? Whaddya like? Baccarat? Roulette?'

'I wouldn't really like to have to choose.' I smiled in the modest manner of an all-round sport who prefers to keep his gambling orgies quiet. It's true that I sometimes bet as much as £1 each way on the Derby and the Grand National.

The small talk remained small. But Perino is not a subtle man. I got the impression that he had been making enquiries at the hotel, to assess my credit rating. Whoever it was to whom he had spoken at the desk must have seen my telex. Perino seemed to be respectful. He started extolling the wonders of Las Vegas, the comforts, the friendly hostesses, the action at the tables.

'For you,' he said gallantly, 'the sky's the limit. I'll tell you what: we have a charter flight leaving Nice Monday. We'd like to have you come along. As our guest, naturally. We'll comp everything in Vegas – hotel, meals, drinks, companionship. All you have to do is sign the tabs.'

'That's very good of you,' I said, keeping any hint of enthusiasm rigorously in check. 'I have to be in Palm Beach for a polo match, but I think I could fit in a week or two in Vegas.'

Most visitors last only three and a half days there.

'Great!' he exclaimed, as if I were doing him a favour.

The flight, via Heathrow and Dublin, was a boisterous one. Stewardesses dressed like Playboy bunnies (the lowest décolletage, the highest black fishnet stockings) served drinks all the way and lobsters and steaks now and then. In the back of the cabin, in a blue haze of cigar and cigarette smoke, there were continuous high-stake games of poker and craps, from which I abstained. I strongly disbelieve in very expensive free flights.

Nevada means 'snow-clad' in Spanish, I read, but climatically it is the driest state in the union. There are deserts and bleached bones. The Spaniards were the first to come to the region where Las Vegas is situated, then the Mormons, then Bugsy Siegel and a large contingent of Mafiosi, then the tourists. Nevada is the most sparsely populated (about half a million inhabitants in 110,540 square miles) but the swingingest of the fifty states. Carson City is the nation's smallest capital, symbolising the Nevadans' premier article of faith, that a little law goes a long way.

Prostitution was introduced to console lonely silver miners

and ranchers and to protect the sheep. It is legal, except in the urban centres, where it would constitute unfair competition with illegal prostitution. There are many amateurs, but they are not true amateurs in the long term. They want to get married. Freeloaders should exercise extreme care, especially when drunk, because neon-lit, cut-price 'wedding chapels' are open for business night and day. In Nevada, one can get married, or, after six weeks' stay to establish residence, divorced, in about as long as it takes to boil an egg.

In Las Vegas, there are chapters of Divorcés Anonymous and Gamblers Anonymous, as well as Alcoholics Anonymous. Divorcés Anonymous sponsor frequent parties for members and other singles, to help them to get married, so that they are qualified to get divorced again. Divorcés like the born-again sensation of getting divorced but they can't get divorced when they are divorcés. The DA parties are only too easy to attend uninvited. They are to be used only *in extremis*.

At meetings of Gamblers Anonymous, gamblers who have been frowned upon by Lady Luck discuss new systems to beat the casinos. No true-blue 'degenerate gambler' (to use the clinical term) is deterred by the fact that a winning system of gambling against the house is a mathematical impossibility. The statistical laws of chance evidently are taught in none of the Nevada public schools, only in closed schools for croupiers. Public awareness of the true odds would be bad for the state economy.

At last the plane landed at McCarran International Airport, and a subdued, frowsty group of high rollers disembarked. I presumed that nobody would be looking for us to start playing right away.

McCarran International Airport was named after the late Senator McCarran. As well as being the author of the McCarran Act, which was intended to restrict the immigration to the United States of anyone politically to the left of Senator McCarthy, Pat McCarran was the senior, often absent partner of McCarran & Kane, the Reno law firm which arranged my first divorce, entirely to the satisfaction of the party of the first part, which was my own self.

I established statutory residence then by spending six weeks in Scotty's Guesthouse, near the University of Nevada campus.

Sprinklers scattered rainbows on smooth lawns. The relationship betweeen Reno and Las Vegas is comparable with that between San Francisco and Los Angeles – snobbishly condescending from north to south and, in the opposite direction, resentfully acrimonious. Reno is of the opinion, valid in my biased judgement, that 'The Biggest Little City In The World', as it calls itself, gets a higher class of divorcés – mostly from the San Francisco area – than Las Vegas, whose divorcés come mostly from Southern California. The rival Nevadan divorce mills indiscriminately share would-be divorcés from the rest of the country, that blank on Nevadan maps known as 'Back East.'

I cannot vouch for the other guesthouses, not having tried any of them yet, but I can testify that Scotty's was ideal for someone maritally disgruntled, fresh out of the Air Force and eager to enter a brave new world.

Scotty, herself a dedicated divorcée who had transcended the whole concept of matrimony, was a middle-aged lady who must have been physically attractive before reaching the age of fifty, which, to me, at that time, seemed old. Having adopted a high-cal diet with fatline tonic water, she wore snug trouser suits in icing-sugar shades of pink, yellow and green, which complemented the dark orange of her hennaed curls. She chainsmoked menthol cigarettes and watched television more than was good for her, but her temperament was sunny. She ran an orderly house, in the sense that it was hygienic. The bedrooms, convivially connected, surrounding a patio and pool, were kept immaculate. However, she believed that women recovering from the stultifying ennui of marriage had the right to do whatever they pleased, as long as they did not make too much noise. There was an encouragingly free-and-easy policy of *laissez-aller* and *laissez-faire*. Anything went.

In a household where women outnumbered men by twentyeight to two while I was an inmate, I felt like a welcome intruder in a harem. The other man, an American ex-marine whose marriage had terminally disimproved during his absence overseas, and I were accorded the privileged status of sheikhs – or better: we were cowboys on a dude ranch without horses. Most of the women had arrived in Reno feeling unloved and sad or angry. They were eager to prove that they were lovable. I, too, was eager to prove that they were lovable. They also felt an irresistible urge to punish their husbands by squandering as much of their money as possible during the six-week climax of marital hostility. There again, easily bearing the light conscience of youth, I was willing to co-operate. The Waring blender was forever whining to produce frozen daiquiris. Lime, pineapple, strawberry and banana were among our favourite flavours.

The guesthouse was almost continuously pulsating with defiant festivities of one kind or another. At times of recuperation, there was a lot of swimming and sunbathing. The scent of a certain coconut suntan lotion still conjures up the slippery, hot, brown skin of afternoons long ago. Freeloaders contemplating a visit to a hostelry for women awaiting divorce should be in the full flush of young personhood.

16

NEEDING to escape from my predatory hosts at the Taj Vegas, I left word at the hotel desk that I had to go to Binion's Horseshoe Hotel & Casino, in Glitter Gulch, downtown Las Vegas. Binion's quaint Western Victoriana, in the oldest part of town, seemed quite cosy after the Taj, not that there was much point in seeking cosiness in that twenty-four-hour city without clocks.

A Binion's staff photographer takes portraits of visitors posing in front of a large horseshoe-shaped showcase containing a million dollars in $10,000 bills. The photographs are printed on postcards, convenient for advertising the establishment in home towns all over the world. The service is free, so, of course, I availed myself of it. Then I left a message to anyone who might ask for me. I said I had been called urgently to return to London.

Now I felt able to make a leisurely tour of the city. I never suffer any pangs of guilt if I disappoint persons who plan to fleece me.

The residential streets of Las Vegas are like middle-income suburban streets anywhere else, but their names are picturesque. Beside the golf course of the Sahara-Nevada Country Club, for example, the names are Indian, such as Mohican, Commanche, Cherokee, Chippewa and Pawnee. Off Paradise Road, between the airport and Paradise Valley, which is as flat as the Great Salt Lake of Utah, there are streets called Count Wutzke, Prince Scotty (a reminder of Reno), Lady Marline, King Richard, Princess Katy, Viscount Carlson and even Sir Patrick. Until then, the address I would have liked best of all was in Toughnut Street, Tombstone, Arizona. But Sir Patrick Street, Las Vegas, augured well: it runs into Gold Dust.

The classified advertisements in *The Las Vegas Sun*, Hank Greenspun's gossip sheet, were revealing. There was one announcing that help was wanted, male, by an 'escort agency'. The pay was good – a hundred and fifty dollars a 'date' and a minimum of five dates a week guaranteed. But another paper reported that the Las Vegas police were investigating local escorts on suspicion of prostitution.

The city authorities do not mind that outsiders call Las Vegas 'Sin City' or 'Lost Wages'. What the authorities mind is the city's reputation for what they call 'sexual rip-offs', the sale of sexual services of insufficient value for money. There are 'sex talk parlours' where men pay women two hundred dollars and up to read aloud from pornographic books.

On the other hand, Las Vegas has far more than its share of religious foundations. There are churches of all the generally known denominations and a number of locally peculiar ones.

The Chapel of Heavenly Bliss is typical of the establishments that specialise in weddings. It is a miniature replica of a colonial church in Concord, Massachusetts, constructed of red brick and white timber. Above the white picket fence there is a sign that lights up at night. It says: 'Instant Weddings Any Time Nite & Day – No   Blood   Test – License – Rings – Music – Flowers – Recordings & Pix.'

The Reverend Mitzi Braun answered the bell. Inside, the chapel was painted pink and gold. The wall-to-wall carpeting was pink. There were two Gothic windows, curved and pointed at the top, covered with pink and yellow cellophane cut in irregular patterns to give the effect of stained glass. Beneath the windows there was a wooden altar, painted yellow, with pale brown imitation grain and knots. A white plaster statue of Cupid, winged, blindfolded, standing on one dimpled foot, with his bow and arrow menacingly poised, occupied the centre of the altar, illuminated by pink electric candles in pink ceramic candelabrums. Seeing that I was staring at Cupid, the minister smiled tenderly.

'The god of love,' she said. 'We are interfaith. Love is for all. We've conducted all varieties of wedding rites here – name it, we've done it. Some couples have ideas of their own. Last week we had a lovely boy and girl who worshipped flying saucers. Why shouldn't they? It's their Constitutional right. Wherever the word 'God' appears in the usual Protestant ceremony – you know, the 'dearly beloved' one – they had 'Venus'. We usually play a tape of 'The Wedding March', but they made their own music, with an ocarina and finger cymbals. We'll go along with anything within reason. But don't let me get started on religion, my pet subject. This is a very beautiful business we're in, but we must always remember to be practical. We must maintain the fabric of the chapel. In that respect, we're like any other church.'

She said that she was qualified to conduct any kind of wedding service. She pointed at a framed parchment certificate on the wall. The certificate was embellished with a red ribbon and a golden paper seal, the official seal of The New Jerusalem Ecumenical Seminary of Burbank, California.

'It's strictly legitimate,' she said. 'We have to do this thing right to stay competitive.'

I cannot overemphasise how careful one has to be in Nevada. The state is rich in opportunities for the enterprising visitor, but there are pitfalls.

When I left The Chapel of Heavenly Bliss, I was feeling a bit depressed. However, in a taxi passing the grand new hotels on The Strip, I noticed that one of the marquees bore the name of the New York comedian I like best of all: Alan King.

I admire Woody Allen. At Michael's Pub in New York where he plays clarinet with a Dixieland group on many a Monday evening, I once told him as he was brooding on the stand between sets that his style reminded me of Johnny Dodds. I had chosen the right name. He was sufficiently pleased to invite me to a private screening of his latest film the following day. But his aphorisms can be discouraging: 'The universe is merely a fleeting idea in God's mind – a pretty uncomfortable thought, particularly if you've just made a down payment on a house.'

Mel Brooks's hysterical scatology can be wearing. Mort Sahl's sardonic monologues are politically defeatist. With Alan King I feel comfortable, and I laugh.

I met him first in London, when he appeared in a Royal Command Performance, then at Les Ambassadeurs for Scotch, then in New York at a Friars Club razzimonial (a dinner in his honour at which all the tributes were turned upside down: 'Alan, you got a lot of polish, but it's all on your shoes'), then in The White Horse Inn, the old English pub that was transported, like a Hearst castle, and rebuilt in Alan's Tudor-style mansion (originally Oscar Hammerstein's) on King's Point, overlooking Long Island Sound, then in a nightclub seating 3,000 in the Concord Hotel in the Catskills, then in Miami Beach, then ... Alan King is friendly.

The first time I visited the Concord, one sunny, crisp winter afternoon, we rode there together, in his chauffeur-driven black Rolls-Royce, drinking whisky from the tubular glass flask, about two and a half feet long, in his hollow malacca cane.

'The first time *I* went up to the Catskills,' he recalled, 'was at the age of thirteen. I ran away from home in Brooklyn and hitch-hiked, taking a few things in a cardboard box tied with string. My parents came and got me, but the next summer they let me return and work. I played drums and sang in funny hats in a four-piece comedy band. I started at the Concord on the staff, as a comic and doing dramatic bits, singing, dancing, setting up chairs, working the lights. All day I was supposed to keep the guests amused. I'd dress in girl's clothes and fall in the pool and do a lot of things like that. I was paid ten dollars a month and room and board.'

He leaned back appreciatively in the soft leather upholstery of the Rolls.

'You heard about the guy at the Wailing Wall in Jerusalem? He's wailing along pretty good there. "I want to be with my people," he wails. "I want to be with my people." "All right, so where are your people?" someone asks. The guy looks surprised, like it's obvious. "At the Concord!"'

'At the height of the summer season,' Alan went on, 'there are more Jews in the Catskills than in the entire State of Israel. No kidding. The women here outnumber the men about nine to one – a lot of secretaries and salesgirls who save their money for fifty weeks for two in the Catskills. The hunting season's open all year round – broads hunting for husbands.' I imagined a super-Scotty's.

He used to work hard at the Concord all summer. Now, for a one-hour show twice a night for a few weeks in Las Vegas, he is paid over a million dollars, plus very lavish expenses. 'I appreciate Vegas for a limited time,' he once said. 'It enables me to do what I always wanted – make money!'

He has not forgotten the early days of arduous apprenticeship.

135

I've never seen him allow a visiting friend to pay for anything.

Caesars Palace (Why no apostrophe? Are apostrophes signs of Eastern effeteness?) is not the newest hotel-casino on The Strip but it is certainly one of the most palatially ornate. The landscaping and decoration of the main approach – the cypresses, the fountains, the dazzling white reproductions of classical statues – might have been inspired by Forest Lawn Cemetery in Los Angeles and the Fountainebleau Hotel (pronounced 'fount'n-bloo') in Miami Beach. A miraculous collaboration of Louis XIV, George IV and Busby Berkeley could not have created anything of more spectacular confectionary enormity.

A porter in the full-dress uniform of a Ruritanian field marshal relieved me of my case, and I used a house phone to find Alan. I found him first beside Frank Sinatra and Andy Williams in a heroes' gallery of giant photographs of regular stars of the supper cabaret in The Circus Maximus, the hotel nightclub. Then I found Alan in the flesh, in a swimsuit, lying on a chaise longue beside the swimming pool, with his face in an aluminium reflector. In Vegas a performer can use suntan instead of pancake make-up. His expression suggested a death mask of a young Rod Steiger as Napoleon. A clear case of solar narcosis.

'This place reminds of The Fountainebleau,' I said.

'Yeah,' he replied, without opening his eyes. 'Why would a fat, middle-aged guy like me want a mirror all over his bedroom ceiling?'

He opened his eyes and said hello.

A New Yorker through and through, Alan says that 'Abroad is a road show.' Everything outside New York, to him, is abroad. When he's away from New York, he sometimes blows his cool and acts sentimental. He shook my hand.

The cabaret was drawing capacity crowds for both the early and late shows. The middle-aged tourist couples who make up a great majority of the audience know Alan as a frequent TV visitor to their living rooms. In the hotel lobby and by the pool, they greeted him with easy familiarity, by his first name.

'For six weeks straight, it's like being on all the time,' he said. 'I'm already looking forward to the peace and quiet of New York, though the day I leave this town is always rough. I'm like a diver coming to the surface too fast; I get the bends.'

I explained why I was a refugee from the Taj Vegas and asked whether there was any chance of his getting me a discount at Caesars.

'You're damn right,' he said. 'I figure they owe me.'

He went up to his room for a rest before getting ready for the evening. When I registered at the desk, I discovered that I had a complimentary suite.

We met before dinner at his private table in The Galleria, a bar near the baccarat tables, on the relatively quiet fringe of the main casino. He always has a few Scotches before the ordeal of the first show.

He looked fresh and cheerful, in black tie and a silk-mohair dinner jacket of Italianate cut. He told anecdotes, some of them New York Jewish, some of them told in the modulated sonority of his W. C. Fields voice, expounding political theory (he's a New Deal Democrat) and discoursing on the philosophy of comedy, now frowning earnestly, now laughing triumphantly, making grandiose gestures with a foot-long Havana cigar.

'Try the hotel's Japanese restaurant for dinner,' he suggested. 'The Ah So. It's a kick. A Japanese restaurant in Vegas. Can you imagine? A little piece of old Kyoto. A memory to cherish always. They're holding a table for you.'

Dinner in the Ah So was an experience of surrealistic wonder. It was as Japanese as Gilbert and Sullivan. A California Nisei, with all the formal grace of a short-order cook in a drugstore, tossed together a fast sukiyaki at my table, while I drank *sake* and gazed bemusedly at a plastic grotto worthy of Walt Disney Productions, bright with artificial flowers and small coloured lights of randomly programmed electronic fireflies.

A few days later, not very well able to return to the Taj Vegas for my return ticket to Monte Carlo, I took a series of air-conditioned buses to Mexico and Guatemala.

17

S PORT can be useful. I'm not talking about darts and snooker, but the more exclusive, up-market, *expensive* recreations, such as yachting and polo. Golf, I acknowledge, has served me well from time to time. I remember tactfully missing an all-important chip and putt on the eighteenth at Killarney. The Japanese visitor was so pleased to win five pounds that he insisted on taking me for a gala dinner at the Europa Hotel – a bargain. Eddie O'Sullivan bought me a pint of Murphy's stout as a reward for having witnessed his birdie on the first at Bantry Park Golf Club. But polo . . .

Iranian tribesmen are said to have played something like polo six hundred years before the birth of Christ. Lieutenant Joseph Sherer, 'The Father of English Polo', began organising the modern game in Calcutta in 1864, after he had seen tribesmen at Silchar, in the north-eastern Indian state of Manipur, playing a fierce mounted contest called *pulu*, the name of the wooden ball they used. Some polo historians say the Tibetans started the game. They gathered each autumn to hunt muskrat. When they found one, they clubbed it to death. If they could not find a muskrat they beat a ball covered with the skin of an animal. Babur, a fifteenth-century Moghul, established the game's popularity in India. Polo has always been associated with royalty, the powerful and the very rich.

By closely studying John Lloyd's definitive book on the subject, *The Pimm's Book of Polo*, I was able to pick up an idea of contemporary polo's social mystique, as well as the basic facts of the game itself, past and present.

There is a revealing chapter by Frank Rohr, 'A Personal View of American Polo', which gives a vivid impression of the state of the art in 1990, the hundredth anniversary of the founding of the United States Polo Association.

According to Mr Rohr, the crucible of corporate sponsorship as it is known today is Palm Beach Polo and Country Club, 'unofficial, and undisputed, world capital of polo.' As set up by its founder, Bill Ylvisaker, with associates like Maggie and Allan Scherer, it was at PBPCC in the 1970s that newly created tournaments such as the $100,000 Piaget World Cup, the Rolex Gold Cup and the Cartier Challenge Cup were shaped and marketed, 'principally to corporations wooing the very rich . . . whose crests then began appearing on the International Field, on team jerseys and in vigorous brand-name national and inter-national promotions.'

The ambience of the clubs, according to Mr Rohr, is 'all horsey catnip to polo cognoscenti,' which includes Yves Piaget, Mollie Wilmot, Ernesto Trotz with Alfonso and Gonzalo Pieres, C. Z. Guest, the Rajmata of Jaipur, TV star Pamela Sue Martin, John Forsythe, Cliff Robertson, 'Bluebook' hostess Mary Sanford, 'hardy playgirl' Zsa Zsa Gabor, George Plimpton, Liz Whitney Tippet, Marylou and C. V. Whitney, film star Jane Seymour . . . 'the usual crowd, darling.'

Mr Rohr hails them among 'the horsey glitterati', who these days include luminaries such as Sylvester Stallone, the hero of the *Rambo* films. I committed the names to memory for casual dropping where they would do most good.

'But for every one of them – because Americans are secret Royalists at heart – the season's ultimate thrill is always a per-sonal and polo-playing visit by Prince Charles, accompanied by his wife the Princess of Wales, still known here [in the United States] as "Lady Di".'

In his enthusiastically commercial introduction to the book, which is a must for the coffee tables of those who wish to seem to be in the know, Major Ronald Ferguson, who was Prince Charles's polo manager, writes:

I have been involved with Pimm's for many years and it gives me great pleasure to be involved with *The Pimm's Book of Polo*. Some years ago I played for a team sponsored by Pimm's. Then as now it seemed fitting that this splendid drink should be seen playing its part in the game. What could be better for player or spectator alike than to enjoy a refreshing glass of Pimm's after a match?

My interest in polo was stimulated further when I read Mr Lloyd's profile of Major Ferguson. 'During his foreign travels he enjoys "fabulous hospitality – and therefore I expect to give of myself in return". One who enjoys his life immensely, Ferguson quips that "most clubs win their matches by their hospitality before the game".' The good major made it quite clear what the fabulous hospitality consisted of, and I wanted some, though without giving of myself in return.

I began by visiting Windsor to watch Prince Charles play on Smith's Lawn, which belongs to the Guards Polo Club. At half-time, spectators are invited to walk up and down the field to tread down the scarred turf. There are royalty-watchers who take part in the ritual in the hope that they will tread the hallowed divots beside the Queen or at least her husband. I also went to watch a match in Cowdray Park, to improve my understanding of the game and the jargon of its aficionados. When one becomes tired of the park, one can nip quickly over to the Spread Eagle in Midhurst.

It was in Paris that polo began to pay off. In Windsor I had overheard a remark about the polo-playing prowess of the renowned restaurateur Claude Terrail, the proprietor of *la Tour d'Argent*. The restaurant seemed reliable, having celebrated its four hundredth anniversary.

I was sitting close to the restaurant's miniature theatre of cuisine, where the *canardier*, in a traditional exhibition of his special skill, was dismembering my duck and flattening it in the hand-operated press, an antique, Heath Robinsonian apparatus, while I was finishing some dainty fish quenelles. Monsieur Terrail, tall, athletic, insouciant, in the course of a routine round of inspection, stopped by my table and asked whether my lunch was satisfactory.

'Eminently,' I assured him. We had never met before, so I had dressed as horsily as possible, in Donegal tweed and cavalry twill. 'The pike is miraculously tender.'

He shrugged, unsurprised. He had heard his quenelles praised thousands of times. But how often had clients praised his polo?

'They tell me your polo backhand is formidable,' I ventured.

The maestro's face was beatified. His smile was rapturous.

'Where did you hear that?'

'Smith's Lawn the other day.'

'Smith's Lawn!' He beamed. 'What are you eating next? The caneton? Excellent. After lunch, you must come backstage, so to speak. I have an apartment through the door there. A brandy then, perhaps?'

A brandy, yes, with pleasure. We had a fine talk – that is to say, Claude told me of stirring combat on the polo fields, and epic parties off the polo fields, of England, France, the United States and Argentina.

'Not only are the Latin Americans the best polo players,' he averred. 'They provide the best *après*-polo amusement.'

The quite substantial cheque I had written in payment for my lunch was never presented to my bank. And on a subsequent visit to Paris, when I returned to the Tour for another numbered duck in the continuing historic series (King Edward VII, as Prince of Wales, ate Number 328, and Princess Elizabeth and Prince Philip in 1948 had Number 185,397 and Number 185,398), I was ushered immediately to the most favoured table, the one by the window with a view of Notre Dame.

There was another lucky break – this time at the communal breakfast table in the dining room of the Chelsea Arts Club – thanks to my new interest in polo. I sometimes drop in to find out about forthcoming openings in London art galleries. As in Taos and, for that matter, anywhere else in the world, the wine served in London galleries as a rule is somewhat plonkish, but much better than nothing.

On this occasion at the club, an American was having breakfast. A cheerful, young fellow. He turned out to be an artist who specialises in caricatures of polo players and flattering portraits of their ponies, as if essaying a synthesis of the works of Spy and Stubbs. He, himself, was a two-goal polo player – not very highly rated, it is true, but with an honourable medical record of broken bones. We had acqaintances in common in Westhampton, Long Island, where he had once run a bar called The Artful Dodger. He said he had recently completed a series of paintings of Prince Charles playing polo in the colours of Guy Wildenstein's *Diables Bleus*, and wondered whether I would like to look them over. I had said nothing to suggest that I was a dealer in the market for polo paintings; however, I had said nothing to suggest that I wasn't.

'Where are they?' I asked.

'Palm Beach. Why don't you come over? You can stay in my place. I have plenty of room.'

I accepted.

The Palm Beach Polo and Country Club, of which, of course, he was a playing member, was crowded the afternoon I attended. Some of the spectators were probably glitterati with famous brand names. These poloists confirmed Frank Rohr's stipulation that 'dress code is blazer and tie, linen suit and real jewellery.' On second thoughts, some of the jewels might have been only replicas of the ones in the vaults, but they looked real enough.

Polo is one of those sports that would be easier to follow on television than in actuality. The field measures 300 yards (three times as long as a football pitch) by 200 yards. When the action is in a distant corner not much can be seen. The most glittering members and guests were drinking in the clubhouse and on its narrow verandah.

My host was engaged in earnest conversation about his Prince Charles equestrian paintings with a Philadelphia dowager who was spending the season at The Breakers, a vast, old-fashioned hotel on the beach, and probably had jewels to spare.

With a proud sense that I was following in the footsteps of one of polo's most aristocratic freeloaders, I applied to the clubhouse bar for a splendid tankard of refreshing Pimm's cup.

I suffered a disappointment.

The drink was served instantaneously, in a small plastic tumbler. It contained no borage, the blue-flowered plant which I had always understood to be a *sine qua non* of Pimm's cup. What would a mint julep be without mint?

I did my best to enjoy the rest of my stay in Palm Beach. But when it was time to leave Las Vegas, I kept in mind Claude Terrail's recommendation of Latin America.

18

M Y revered mentor Vincent Overly, in our instructive confabulations, has often emphasised that luck is not mere happenstance. One of the important first principles of freeloading is that *one must make one's own luck*, by exposing oneself, as often as can be contrived, to the possibility of being 'entertained'.

True patriots, particularly those who are well-to-do, always welcome opportunities to display the beauties and comforts of their countries to appreciative visiting foreigners. I can say in all (reasonable) humility that I never allow false pride to inhibit me from offering myself as a fully committed guest.

In Guatemala City, I stayed at the Pan American Hotel while getting my bearings.

At the earliest opportunity I went to watch a polo match. Guatemala were playing Costa Rica. Here were people who convened on a polo ground for the sake of polo. Guatemala won. At the party afterwards, I was introduced to Jorge Luna. The President of the Jockey Club of Guatemala and an indefatigable polo player, he, like the three other members of his team and their supporters, was in a state of incandescent ebullience. Happy is the word. In no longer than it takes to play a chukka (seven minutes) we were on the best of terms.

We talked of polo and polo players and the places where polo is played. His wife had been one of Guatemala's showjumping team in the Montreal Olympics. More recently, he had jumped and played polo for his country in Europe and North America. He had not met Claude Terrail; however, the world of polo being small, Jorge had heard of him, and was pleased to hear his high opinion of polo in Latin America. Chains of compliments and goodwill can be unending.

'The food in Guatemala isn't too bad,' Jorge said. 'I'll pick you up at your hotel tomorrow evening at eight.'

146

I was waiting on the pavement outside the hotel at 8.00, at 8.05, 8.10 and 8.15. Guatemalans have an Irish sense of time, so all was well. At 8.25, a silver-grey Alfa Romeo snarled up the street and squealed to a stop beside me.

'We have a table at El Patio,' Jorge said. 'But we have plenty of time on the way for an apéritif.'

Before midnight we were eating T-bone steaks of Texan dimensions. He said:

'You don't have to stay in the city, do you?'

His father had been a landowner in the fertile sugar-cane country near Santa Lucia Cotzumalguapa, in the Pacific lowlands. The family had experienced economic reverses during Jorge's childhood, but, like his father, Jorge appreciated land, not only as property but as a basis of emotional security. He had made a lot of money importing heavy machinery from the United States to Guatemala City, but he still felt like a countryman. He had recently acquired a coffee *finca* near the old family farm, and had bulldozed enough acreage to make a polo field. He had also established a stud to breed polo ponies.

'Well,' he said, 'where do you want to stay?'

I said I hoped to be able to look around.

'I have a house at Lake Atitlán,' he said. 'That's a nice place. You can use the house as a base. Stay there as long as you like. I don't go there often. As a matter of fact, I have a couple of houses there, not too close together. We wouldn't get in each other's way. There's a car you can borrow. It's an old Plymouth but it goes all right. I'll send it over in the morning.'

And there was more.

'Cruz has the key to the boat,' he said.

'Cruz?'

'Cruz Lopez is the houseboy. Houseman – he's in his fifties now. He has his own place there, near your house. He can show you how everything works. He's very good.'

'There'll be someone with me,' I said. 'Her name's Diana.'

'OK! I was going to ask you whether you are a cook.'

Although only the size of Wales, Guatemala, because of its subtropical latitude and its extreme vertical variations, from steamy sea-level rainforest to frosty alpine peaks above 10,000 feet, offers a remarkable variety of climates. There is a rainy season, from May to November, and a dry season. In the rainy season, the rain falls heavily but briefly and punctually at the end of every afternoon. In the dry season there is hardly any rain at any time. Both seasons are delightful, justifying the Tourist Commission's sobriquet, 'The Land of Eternal Spring'. Lake Atitlán, almost a mile above sea level, enjoys the best climate of all, all year. At the lake, it is always warm enough at midday for comfortable swimming, and cool enough at night for log fires and blankets.

A little more than eleven miles long, from east to west, and four miles wide, and as much as a thousand feet deep, the lake was created an unknown number of thousands of years ago, when volcanic upheavals sealed the river exits from a broad highland valley surrounded by mountain peaks. Four volcanoes, now inactive, are grouped fairly close together on the lake's south shore. The locally prevailing southerly winds accumulate towering clouds over these blue-green volcanic cones, attaining climactic formations every evening in time to make sunset-watching one of the most rewarding local activities, comparable with flower- and butterfly-watching.

Pedro de Alvarado, the sixteenth-century Spanish *conquistador*, brought Mexican Indian troops with him when he invaded Guatemala, and they gave the lake its present name. Atitlán means 'place of much water'. The water is as pure and clear and good to drink as Malvern's. The lake contains enough water for a legendary monster, and to accommodate the innumerable ghosts of the drowned, who are said to beckon enticingly to the living to join them. Lake Atitlán is certainly hard to leave.

J. L. Stephens, a nineteenth-century American explorer, wrote of the lake in his *Incidents of Travel in Central America, Chiapas and Yucatan*: 'We [he and his English travelling companion and illustrator, Frederick Catherwood] both agreed that it was the most magnificent spectacle we ever saw.'

Aldous Huxley, never an easy man to impress, admired the colours of the lake and was reminded of Italy, the classic standard by which he measured other countries' landscapes. He called Lake Atitlán 'Lake Chromo'.

Any traveller conscientiously doing his best to compile a definitive list of The Ten Most Beautiful Views in the World would have to give Jorge's view of Lake Atitlán serious consideration.

The point I am trying to make is that Lake Atitlán is the most beautiful place in which I have ever lived. The view can be compared with the view from Patjo Daly's bar in Ahakista, West Cork, across the garden and the waters of Dunmanus Bay to the hills of the Mizen Head peninsula – enlarged, in tropical colours.

Jorge apparently had lost count of the buildings he had constructed at the lake. There was a main house like a Swiss chalet, a guesthouse, a house for each of his two daughters, a house for his servants, a studio, an open pavilion for a barbecue and a ping-pong table and an Indian-style sauna bathhouse. There were two wooden jetties for his cabin cruisers.

The terraced hillside gardens were shaded by eucalyptus, avocado, orange, lime and palm trees, and gaudy with red and pink hibiscus and orchids and magenta and scarlet bougainvillaea. There were hummingbirds. As Keats, on an up day, put it quite neatly:

> *What is more gentle than a wind in summer?*
> *What is more soothing than the pretty hummer*
> *That stays one moment in an open flower,*
> *And buzzes cheerily from bower to bower?*

Time is magical at the lake. The hours at first seem to pass very slowly. Then somehow they begin to melt and slip by in a hypnotic flux that softens and distorts timepieces, so that they sag limply like the watches in Dali's painting, *The Persistence of Memory*. Suddenly days become months. It is not uncommon for foreign visitors to come for a holiday and stay for the rest of their lives.

A typical day began at seven o'clock, when the sun rose above the ridge of the mountain beside the house. The sun quickly evaporated the haze over the volcanoes. It was worth getting up to watch the sunrise colours of the lake – oyster-grey and pale peach ripples with crests of mercurially dazzling silver.

After swimming and not watching the news on television (no television) and not reading the news in the newspaper (no newspaper), we breakfasted usually on papaya with slices of lime and local dark honey, ham and eggs, brown bread and butter and guava jelly, and several cups of Antigua coffee, which

James Bond would have preferred to Jamaican Blue Mountain, if only he had travelled a bit farther.

Swinging gently in a hammock in leafy shade, listening to the soft rush of waves washing the beach and to the muted wooden chimes of the marimba in the Indian village across the bay, I thought of the Mayans.

Guatemalans seem to experience a sense of bereavement when they contemplate the great, remote, impersonal loss of the Mayan civilisation. It reached its apotheosis in what is now Guatemala, and then, about a thousand years ago, suddenly fell. Exactly how and why, nobody knows.

The Mayan achievement was tremendous. But evidently it was obsessively specialised, perhaps fatally so. As in some other civilisations, what began as functionalism ended in ornament, ritual and speculation. The astronomer-priests – the élite of an increasingly top-heavy theocracy – apparently were men of marvellous but limited cleverness. They devised complex systems of hieroglyphics and calendrics. They learned how to time planetary motion to the second. They were sufficiently sophisticated intellectually to invent zero, but too specialised to put the circle to work as the wheel. And then there were all those sacrifices, cutting out people's hearts to supply the gods with enough blood and benevolence to raise the sun each morning. After a number of centuries, the practice undoubtedly lost much of its original charm, and almost all its popularity. And then? An unusual water shortage? A series of poor crops? A debilitating epidemic? A tactless sermon? Revolution? Migration? The end is guesswork.

I opened my eyes with an effort, in time for another swim and the happy hour. Jorge had told me where he kept the drink and urged me to help myself. His favourite tipple was Scotch. I wanted to try the drink of the country.

The national drink of Guatemala is a sugar-cane distillate called *aguardiente*. It is absolutely colourless, without even the lovely, wistful, pale blue glint of gin. The Spanish portmanteau word means 'ardent water'. It has the ardour of an open-hearth blast furnace and the passion of napalm. The object of its searing love is the juice of the human body. So powerful is *aguardiente*'s affinity for the moist essences of the person, in fact, that the unwary, immoderate drinker of it risks being reduced almost instantaneously to a small terracotta doll, dehydrated to the dry powder of instant hangover. On Guatemalan market days the rural ditches are terribly populous with Indians seized in the grotesque rigid postures of invaders in the snow around Stalingrad. In short, *aguardiente* is a drink that the prudent eschew.

The Guatemalans mercifully also distil a credible light rum in the style of white Bacardi. Jorge gave me a recipe which I used to enhance the joy of watching the sun set. A Coffee Blossom, as he called it, is made like a daiquiri, with the addition of a small quantity of fresh pineapple juice and a touch of concentrated syrup of coffee. One level teaspoon of Nescafé to each double-size cocktail will do.

Although they are still sad about the demise of the mighty Mayans, Guatemalans are admirable, even enviable, in their attitude towards the death of individuals. They regard death as a member of the family. They are at once sentimental and calmly practical.

There is an undertaker's shop in Antigua, the old Spanish Colonial capital, characteristically called *El Dulce Sueno*, The Sweet Sleep. You can usually hear the brisk rasp of the carpenters' saws there and the knock of their hammers, for there is a steady demand for coffins, many of them very small.

The funeral processions are cathartically emotional. I once followed pallbearers who were already reeling with *aguardiente* on the way to the cemetery and weeping so uninhibitedly that their sobs sounded close to hysterical laughter. The widow knew they really cared. Only in Ireland had I witnessed such a sensible, cheerful cortège, expressing such faith.

Though it may not merit the classification of freeloading (but if not, why not?), one of my happiest experiences in Guatemala during that six-month sojourn was Thanatotic. All Saints' Day is one long rocket barrage of salutes and a musical saturnalia, as well as a day to go to church. On the next day, the Day of the Dead, the men, women and children of three, even four, generations enjoy a communal reunion picnic among the pastel-washed, stuccoed tombstones. In the large cemetery at Sololá, Lake Atitlán's provincial capital, I saw an ice-cream vendor selling an ice-cream cone to a happy mourner carrying a wreath. They believed in heaven.

An Indian family, grandmother, mother and father and four

151

children, invited me to join them for lunch on the base of a pale orange mausoleum in which several of their antecedents were already at rest. There was an abundance of food and drink, with plenty of cakes and chocolates for the children.

I didn't feel at all like Malcolm Lowry's miserable Consul in *Under The Volcano*.

M ANY owners of private planes who would never consider
stopping their cars to pick up hitchhikers are quite willing
to give strangers lifts by air. It is necessary only that the strangers
should be sufficiently well groomed and seem to be travelling
for fun. Nobody obviously in need of help is very likely to get
it.

Wearing a quietly dapper new Panama hat, impractically large
sunglasses with bamboo frames, a yellow linen blazer and so
forth, I took a taxi early one morning to Guatemala's Aurora
Airport. (Diana had already flown home by orthodox means. I
was heading in a different direction for the time being.) At
the Operations tower, I enjoyed a chat with one of the flight
controllers. I asked him respectful questions about his interesting, important work. He provided us with coffee, and allowed
me to look at the flight plans that had been filed so far that day.
As usual at that busy airport, several private planes were bound
for the United States. I noted a few of the more promising ones
that were going to Florida.

A short stroll in the sunshine brought me face to face with
the right sort of pilot. Guillermo Lucas, a millionaire *fincero*
(coffee planter), was about to fly his Gulfstream to Miami. Space
for a passenger? A passenger with a dapper new Panama hat and
a Concorde bag?

'*Hombre! Si, como no?*' Why not?

Culturally Miami leaves something to be desired. By a city's signs
you shall know it. On the way to Collins Avenue, Miami Beach's
most fashionable thoroughfare, where the land is so expensive
and the buildings are constructed so close together that from
the shoreline road you cannot see the sea. I saw a cultural
pathologist's collectors' items: The Yacht Upholstery Shoppe,

154

Dog Obedience Consultant, Copa City – 50 Beautiful Twistettes and The Stuft Shirt Lounge.

Back in Miami proper, I encountered a Cuban in overalls carrying on his shoulder a large wooden cross.

'What for?' I asked him, thinking that he was a penitent who was planning to punish himself too severely.

'A hunnert bocks,' he replied in a businesslike tone of voice.

'A hundred dollars!'

'*Si*. Is carvèd by hand. Is hand carvèd.'

Seeking spiritual refreshment, I went to the office of the Drug Enforcement Adminstration and learned the name of the narcotics agents' neighbourhood bar.

There were several of them there, easily recognisable as such because of their outrageous disguises. A few of them were dressed with the flashy designer informality of Don Johnson in *Miami Vice*. Others looked like the skippers of powerboats, who, to mingle with the smugglers, needed only eye patches, peg legs and parrots.

I introduced myself and was welcomed most cordially. These men are hungry for a friendly word. They are accustomed to the rebuffs of members of the local business community, who feel that the activities of the DEA are harmful to trade.

My accent immediately gave me away, of course. The agents are trained observers.

'Don't tell us,' said one of the younger men, a Don Johnson lookalike with three days' nicely trimmed black stubble, wearing a white T-shirt and a white linen suit about three sizes too loose. 'Let us guess. You're from Scotland Yard, right? The Central Drugs Intelligence Unit?'

I raised a finger to my lips, winked, and otherwise in body language subtly bade him exercise discretion. The agent respected my request for confidentiality, indicating his willingness to co-operate by gently nudging me in the ribs and buying me an ice-cold bottle of Beck's beer.

'Gene Francar of our Lauderdale office has been working with one of your guys down in the Turks and Caicos Islands,' another agent said, to make me feel that I was among confederates. 'Hey, what's with your people in London? How come they let Norman Saunders, the Chief Minister of the Colony, refuel the drug smugglers' planes from Colombia like that for so long?

What was that supposed to be? He was commuting to Miami every week with a caseful of thousand-dollar bills.'

I winked again, looked around the bar, and winked once more.

'A trap, huh?' an agent suggested, buying me another beer.

'I'm going over to the Bahamas,' I said. 'Can you fellows give me any helpful leads?'

Almost all of them spoke at once. They recommended all sorts of people, from the Prime Minister, Sir Lynden O. Pindling, down and sideways, from New Providence Island to many of the Out Islands of the 730-island archipelago.

'You can make good contacts on the closest island of all,' one of the agents promised. 'I think you'd like Bimini. Try the Compleat Angler.'

Chalk's International Airline, which was founded in 1919 and claims plausibly to be the oldest airline in the world, took me, and sixteen other passengers, in one of the world's oldest airliners. The Grumman Mallard is an antique flying boat whose twin propellers, as quaintly old-fashioned as hand-turned egg whisks, stir thoughts of the distant epoch when flying was one of the luxurious privileges of a small, eccentric minority. An amphibian, it took off from Florida using its wheels and came down on its broad, white hull in a hiss of spray on the far edge of the dark blue Gulf Stream. Then the Mallard lowered its wheels again and waddled ashore, up a ramp to a one-room Customs & Immigration building, where baggage and passport inspection was cursory.

Bimini was British for three hundred and forty-four years, until 1973. Queen Elizabeth is still the Queen of the Commonwealth of the Bahamas. The new coat of arms depicts a swordfish and a flamingo supporting a picture of Christopher Columbus's flagship, *Santa Maria,* surmounted by a blazing sun, an aphrodisiac conch, and palms. The new Bahamian motto is 'Forward, Upward, Onward Together.'

The Customs and Immigration officers, like members of the Bahamian police and defence forces, continue to wear uniforms of British design, as the Speaker of the Bahamas House of Assembly in Nassau wears a shoulder-length grey woollen wig, like the Speaker's in the House of Commons. Such vestigial insignia of colonial status help to give visiting Americans that amusing *abroad* feeling, add colour to home movies, and create an illusion of security.

There is another, more fundamental heritage from the Bahamas' colonial years. It is a matter of temperament and attitude. While the Bahamas retain the panoply and ritual of English common law, many Bahamians now, as always, proudly flout law of every kind. If they are not hard pressed, they usually laugh about what they are doing. By nature, they are genial. But they do not take kindly to any authority. They are inviolably unservile. If they don't like instructions or the way they are given, Bahamians will go to any lengths and take immense trouble to disobey.

Bahamians were independent even before Independence. Now they are more independent than ever. Now, as always, the Bahamas is a nation of pirates, smugglers and bootleggers. Their anti-authoritarian sense of vocation has not wavered since they plundered the bullion ships of the Spanish Main, ran arms to the American South during the Civil War, and supplied booze to the whole Union during the years of Prohibition.

Nowadays the commodities of illicit trade through the Bahamas are much more valuable and dangerous, and the traditional anarchic spirit is more vigorously defiant than ever before. A nation that produces next to nothing has to hustle. As Americans are the Bahamas' best customers, Bimini, only fifty miles off the coast of Florida, is the hustlers' most convenient base.

The islands of Bimini, North and South, are two of the smaller inhabited islands of the Bahamas. Bimini's total land area is only nine square miles, with a resident population of about 1,500. There is a large number of transients, many arriving in their own boats, which may or may not be used for fishing.

Ponce de Leon was looking for Bimini in 1513, in his search for the Fountain of Youth, but missed the place and landed in Florida instead. Before there was any danger of his growing old, Indians killed him.

On Bimini actuality and speculation often seem inextricably intermixed. What is history, what is legend? So many big fish get away. It isn't that people on Bimini deliberately bend the truth more than the people do anywhere else. But sunshine and rum and other mind-transformers are sometimes hallucinogenic.

Even if there is a magical fountain on South Bimini, as it has been hinted, no effort has been made to exploit it as a tourist attraction. But the inhabitants of South Bimini are noted for their ability to keep their ambition in check. They are laid far back. In Alice Town, on North Bimini, it is said that once when a hurricane cut off the southern island's electricity many months passed before anybody noticed. On North Bimini they probably would have noticed before the end of the first week.

Ossie Brown's hotel, the Compleat Angler, is only a few hundred yards along the road from where the flying boat came ashore. A simple, three-storey, twelve-bedroom, wood-frame structure close to the road, with a giant almond tree in the patio, the hotel is celebrated, as a sign on the side of the building proclaims, as 'The Home of Papa Ernest Hemingway'.

Hemingway slept around even more than George Washington, but it is true that the author stayed in the hotel a lot of the time, from the year it opened, in 1935. The management claims he wrote *Islands in the Stream*, his last novel, while he was living there. The hotel is well situated, across the road from Bimini dock, and was well suited to his needs. It has no dining room but there is a dimly lighted, no-frills bar, which is still the centre of Alice Town's piscatorical social life. There are photographs of Hemingway with friends and blue marlin on the walls of a Hemingway Memorial Room. It is a ruggedly masculine room, like a North American backwoods hunting lodge, with dark panelling, a large fireplace, dark red leather armchairs and backgammon tables.

The collection of photographs includes one of *Pilar*, the cabin cruiser in which Hemingway searched in local waters and the Caribbean for German submarines during World War Two. Among her important specifications was her capacity to carry 2,400 pounds of ice. Another picture, a caricature of machismo, shows Papa standing on the dock, firing a Thompson submachine-gun from the shoulder.

Lately, a caption explains in his own words, *we have been using a Tommy gun on sharks when they come after hooked fish.* He tempted sharks to jump out of the water after bait and then let them have short bursts, in his usual style, good and true.

When I gave my name to the man at the hotel desk, he said: 'Sure. We got a call to expect you.'

I wondered whether one of the DEA agents had telephoned to help me or to warn the management.

'We're giving you a room we think you'll like,' the desk clerk said.

After checking in, I went for a walk, with brief stops at the Crazy Gregg Saloon, the Bloody Mary Bar, the Fisherman's Paradise, the Pirates' Den and the End of the World Bar. But the best was Brown's Hotel, owned by Ossie Brown's brother, Neville. The bar had a sign saying, 'Prices Subject to Change Depending on Attitude of Customer'.

'You're Mr Catling,' the bartender said. Maybe it was Neville.

The drinks were on the house. Another telephone call, of course.

I wanted to buy some stamps. The post office was open, but there was nobody there. A boy passing by said that Commissioner Stubbs had the key, and that the Commissioner was in his house next door, resting.

Commissioner Wilton Stubbs welcomed me. Before we got around to the subject of stamps, he told me about his visit to Nassau to testify before a Royal Commission investigating the drugs traffic between Colombia and the United States by way of the Bahamas.

'I told those people in Nassau that eighty per cent of our kids above the age of fourteen were using cocaine,' he said with a smile.

'Eighty per cent!' I exclaimed. 'That's a lot. Where did you get that figure?'

He chuckled.

'It's really a hundred per cent, but I didn't want to alarm them.'

I was in my hotel bedroom, preparing to sleep, hoping for gratifying rapid-eye-movement episodes, when I heard voices in the next room. The wooden wall between me and them was thin. They were speaking Spanish, which I do not fully understand without wine and music. But even Don Johnson in his simple-minded detective mode would have understood that they were from Barranquilla, on the northern coast of Colombia, and that they were talking about a trip to Fort Lauderdale, not on vacation.

The next morning I checked out.

There was no bill.

I messed about in Nassau quite pleasurably for a while, though without any outstanding success in terms of this treatise. My only major gain was not, strictly speaking, free.

In a hotel casino, I happened to hear the manager of the hotel parasail concession say he needed a man to ride a parasail while fully dressed in ordinary street clothes, rather than the usual swimsuit, for publicity purposes – to show how easy it is. A parasail is like the umbrella of a parachute. The rider, attached to it by a harness, is pulled by a speedboat and caused to fly about a hundred to a hundred and fifty feet high, like the tail of a giant kite. When the boat slows down, the parasail naturally descends. Of course it *is* very easy; no skill is required. I was qualified for the job.

'Excuse me,' I said, in the eavesdropper's conventional opening gambit, 'but I couldn't help overhearing you . . .'

Like Major Ferguson, I didn't really give of myself; I sold of myself. For my ten minutes of parasailing, which was a bracing experience, quite enjoyable in its ghastly, vertiginous way, the hotel gave me a complimentary ground-floor room, with French windows opening on to Emerald Beach, and meals, for a week.

Walking along Bay Street, the main street, one morning, I was exposed to a good idea, which I wouldn't mind passing on, for what it's worth.

20

B AY Street is both mysterious and blatantly obvious, running
the gamut of high-profit enterprises from Government
offices and the House of Assembly to tourist-trap bars – not a
lengthy gamut.

There's a statue of Queen Victoria opposite Rawson Square.
There's a straw market (now ignominiously mostly concealed),
where tough, genial mammies sell hats, handbags and dolls of
woven straw decorated with multicoloured raffia. There are
shops that specialise in perfume, cashmere and booze. As in
Vaduz, Liechtenstein, there are many brass wall plaques repre-
senting the registered imaginary offices of foreign corporations
avoiding foreign taxes. Bay Street gave the old white oligarchy
that ran the colony its innocent-sounding name, 'The Bay Street
Boys'. Harold Christie must often giggle in his grave.

In the window of a newly established real-estate office, there
was an eye-catching, imagination-inflaming invitation to make
'The Investment of a Lifetime' – in Christopher Columbus. It is
significant that the statue in front of what used to be the most
important building in Nassau – Government House – is of
Christopher Columbus, one of the most outstanding salesmen
of all time.

'Come in!' a notice urged me. 'We will take you, absolutely
free and without obligation, to inspect choice sites for residential
and commercial development on Christopher Columbus Island,
the beautiful, unspoilt island of San Salvador. Come and find out
about magnificent, never-to-be-repeated opportunities! Weekly
visits – ALL EXPENSES PAID.'

I had always resisted without difficulty the temptation to
succumb to the blandishments of London estate agents who
offer free trips to prospective purchasers of time-share villas on
the Costa del Crime and various other congested garden spots

162

on the polluted shore of the Mediterranean. San Salvador, however, seemed different.

Having hurriedly returned to my hotel to change from the yellow blazer of a happy-go-lucky *bon vivant* to the navy blue of a serious prospective purchaser, I entered the real-estate office and signed up for the earliest possible inspection trip.

Christopher Columbiana is going to be the hottest commodity of the 1990s. Membership will boom in America's Knights of Columbus. Rents will go up around New York's Columbus Circle. Tourists will throng to Columbus, in North Dakota, Georgia, Indiana, Kansas, Mississippi, Montana, Nebraska, New Jersey, New Mexico, Ohio, Texas and Wisconsin. On a grander international scale, Colombian drug barons with a sentimental sense of history will distribute free lines of coke. The chambers of commerce of Genoa, Seville and the Canary Islands will go into overdrive. But nowhere can entrepreneurs be more glowingly optimistic about dealing in Christopher Columbus futures than in the Bahamas. And where entrepreneurs are buoyed up by optimism, freeloaders may be confident of finding the main chance.

San Salvador Island, about halfway down the windward fringe of the Bahamas island chain, is where the New World officially began. Bahamian Independence Day, as celebrated at the United Nations, may be 10 July, but the Bahamas' most important national holiday, surely, must be 12 October.

The twelfth of October 1492, was the day The Great Navigator blundered into the Americas. He is said to have taken one celestial fix all the way across the Atlantic, and evidently he was all thumbs with the astrolabe: the fix was wildly aberrant, indicating that his tiny fleet was cruising in the region of the latitude of Labrador, on what he had promised his Spanish royal sponsors was the scenic route to China.

The Arawaks or Lucayans who lived on the island in the fifteenth century called it Guanahani. There's a housing estate in Nassau named after it. When Columbus came ashore he gratefully kissed the beach and renamed the island San Salvador. He felt saved from his nervous sailors' mutinous grumbling after too many days at sea. Some of the Arawaks paddled dugout canoes to meet the ships. Others met the leaders of the expedition on the beach. The Arawaks thought at first (not for long) that the strangers were gods. Columbus, disoriented by many thousands of miles, thought the Arawaks were Indians.

There was an exchange of gifts: Spanish glass beads and other trinkets for Arawak parrots, darts and skeins of cotton. Columbus was favourably impressed by the agreeable manners of the 'Indians'. He asked them politely where they got their gold. The Arawaks, possibly misunderstanding the question, pointed to Rum Cay.

In his log, Columbus wrote that the Arawaks 'love their neighbours as themselves, and their speech is the sweetest and gentlest in the world, and they always speak with a smile.' Then he thoughtfully added: 'They should be good servants.'

In a report to Queen Isabel, he suggested: 'When Your Highnesses so command, they can all be carried off to Castille or held captive in the island itself, since with fifty men they would all be kept in subjection and forced to do whatever may be wished.' Thus Europe's Upstairs-Downstairs philosophy was introduced to the new continent.

The present population of San Salvador is descended mostly from African slaves, privateers, pirates and planters, Loyalists who moved to the Bahamas after the American Revolution and a miscellany of more recent migrants from Europe and the Americas.

When I made my landfall, I found that San Salvadorans today are of many hues – black, brown, beige (Ellington again) and those boiled-lobster colours which some Caucasians turn when exposed to fair weather. The present ethnic mixture is much more complex than that of the Arawaks Columbus met. But environment may be more influential than heredity. The Bahamian sunshine, the deep cobalt of the Bahamian sky, the indigo and turquoise of the Bahamian sea and the soft warmth of the white Bahamian beaches exert a wonderful benefaction on most of the people who live there. More often than not, like the gentle Arawaks, modern San Salvadorans speak with a smile.

It was not immediately easy to perceive what the island gave them to smile about. Inland, it didn't at first seem to be much. The land remains much the same as it was in 1831, when Charles Farquharson, one of the more successful planters of his day, described his property as 'mostly pond, scrub and bare rock'.

Like some other underdeveloped Bahamian islands, our

hard-selling escort told us, 'San Salvador has great potential wealth that may be realised in the near future with startling suddenness. Think Columbus, and look at the beaches.' He showed us a video of sand and sea and a map of available building sites, so I excused myself from the Riding Rock Inn, managed by the Columbus Landings Company, to look at the realities.

Looking out to sea and beneath it, I saw there was a sound basis for the enthusiasm of Columbus's journal. 'There are here fish,' he wrote, 'so unlike ours it is a marvel ... of the finest colours in the world, blue, yellow, red and of all colours, and others painted in a thousand ways, and the colours are so fine that no man would not wonder at them or be anything but delighted to see them.' Old C. C. wrote as well as he navigated.

Dr Doris Johnson, who was President of the Bahamian Senate and Chairman of the Discovery Day Festival Committee, announced long ago how she wanted to pay tribute to Columbus. When her committee installed an underwater bronze marker to show where Columbus may have dropped anchor for the first time in the New World, she said the next phase of the memorial would be a 'Peace Light, the same height as the Washington Monument in Washington'.

Dr Johnson said the edifice upholding the Peace Light would be big enough to contain a hotel and a restaurant.

Walking barefoot along the empty beach, I envisioned even bigger developments on the long-neglected island. With the support of the Bahamian Ministry of Tourism, the Out Island Promotion Board and the Inter-American Development Bank, San Salvador before long will very likely have a thirty-mile ring of beachfront hotels and condominiums to rival those of Miami Beach.

And a casino. The Christopher Columbus Casino.

I expect the management to invite me to the gala opening.

21

HERE at last came a chance for me to do something to show my gratitude to the old master. Vincent needs no assistance from me, but I was glad to be able to make a small gesture. How was I to foresee that what started out small would turn into something quite big?

I was rather despondently house-sitting in Montpelier Square for some friends last March. They, of course, were in their house in the Lyford Cay compound in the Bahamas. I'm not really complaining; I like Montpelier Square; the Richard Kilians had left me well provided for, and the cat left voluntarily. I enjoy walking over to Harrods to browse in the Food Hall. The patterned ensembles of fish on marble are exquisite, and the cheeses are usually sensibly arranged. But, well, you know what March in London can be like if you are not deeply in love. It's a month that can drag. This year I felt the cold. Nobody was smiling much.

However, one morning I overcame my lethargy and succeeded in getting out of bed well before opening time. I took a taxi to St James's, to see whether my wine merchant could come up with any helpful bargains in the way of old château-bottled clarets. I was conducting yet another of my periodic economy campaigns. I don't find scrimping easy, but fortunately I am no wine snob. The claret doesn't have to be Latour, Margaux or Lafite-Rothschild every time.

Geoffrey (my merchant and I have been on first-name terms as long as I can remember) told me about a wine tasting that was to be held in the City the following day. I attend many wine tastings, both at home and abroad, and always call in to sample the wares of wineries when on holiday in their vicinity.

Some of the tastings are now rather blurred in the memory; but some of them are unforgettable. For instance, I remember the time when John Gilbey kindly invited me to the feast for the vignerons on the Gilbey estate in Bordeaux one St Vincent's Day. St Vincent, it will be recalled, is the patron saint of workers in vineyards – a fact that gives Vincent Overly confidence every time he draws a cork. The Gilbeys assembled in a salon of their château at noon the day after the banquet. We sat around gazing at each other in silence for a while. 'I don't know about you people,' John said eventually, responsibly assuming the intiative, 'but I don't think more red wine ... I'm going to have a large vodka.' My eyes filled with tears of gratitude.

'Tomorrow should be interesting,' Geoffrey said. 'There's going to be a blind tasting of Rhenish wines, including some wines from Australia. Dr Adzug is in London. He'll be there.'

I was bound to admit that I had never heard of Dr Adzug. Geoffrey couldn't help raising his eyebrows. People in wine, be they merchants, sommeliers or those non-productive, professional oenologists who only write about it, often expect laymen to share their knowledge. I am almost a *chevalier de tastevin*, but I don't pretend to know everything about the subject. I'm not the sort of person who would go about flashing a chevalier's silver tasting cup.

'Dr Stefan Adzug is the leading wine producer in the Barossa Valley, in South Australia,' Geoffrey explained. 'He is said to be one of the most knowledgeable, *wealthiest* viniculturists in the world. His doctorate from the University of Adelaide is in the psychology of ergonomics. The experts of the Kaiser Stuhl co-operative and Hardy's Yalumba, two of the region's most highly regarded wine producers, go to Dr Adzug for advice. He owns one of Australia's premier racing stables. He'll probably get at least a knighthood in the Birthday Honours List. There is talk in the wine trade that Robert Redford has asked to play him in a major motion picture about synthetically enhanced fermentation.'

'Gosh,' I said.

I telephoned Vincent.

'Glad tidings,' I told him. 'There's an interesting blind tasting of Rhine wines tomorrow. There's an Australian wine man, a Dr Adzug – '

'Hold on a second. I'm just going to turn down the Art Tatum.'

Vincent quickly returned to the telephone.

'Did you say Dr Adzug? *The* Dr Adzug? Steve Adzug?'

Vincent agreed to meet the next morning in The Lamb for a preparatory snort and then to proceed together to the cellars.

That afternoon I brushed up my German wine terminology. From André Simon I got *Originaabfullung*, meaning bottled by the grower. My well-thumbed Postgate contributed *Goldbeerenauslese,* meaning that only the ripest grapes on each bunch were used. At drinks time, I called on good old Cyril Ray in his apartment in Albany. He was just opening a bottle of Chambéry, to which I have always been partial. It went down smoothly and was not at all liverish.

'*Trockenbeerenauslese* is a jolly good word to have in your quiver,' Cyril said. 'It means more or less the same as *Goldbeerenauslese*, but, being three letters longer, is more convincing proof that you know your stuff.'

Wearing my lucky, unstainable wine-tasting tie, purple silk, loosely knotted, I arrived at my rendezvous with Vincent on the dot.

Because it was Vincent, I bought us a drink. And because it was Vincent I demurred for an instant when he reciprocated.

'I want to get there a little ahead of time,' I said. 'There is, I fancy, the embryo of a wheeze.'

He nodded approvingly.

We got to the cellars, with grimy brick walls that must have been a yard thick. In a long, underground vault with an arched ceiling, a refectory table, covered with a snow-white linen cloth, bore a row of shrouded bottles and many glasses. Our host was already there, of course, a solemn but friendly man with an experienced vintner's complexion of bruised mauve and pale scarlet, which was well displayed above a stiff white collar. He was dressed like a barrister, in a black jacket and striped black and grey trousers.

'The others should be along presently,' he said. 'Perhaps you would care for a glass of hock while you're waiting. To get tuned up, as it were.'

Leaving Vincent to beguile the vintner for a couple of minutes, and nobody in London is better than Vincent when it comes to beguilement, I took the green-aproned cellarman aside into a farther corner of the long, fragrant vault.

He, too, had the colouring of a long, intimate love affair with the grape. I did not mince words, and I preliminarily sweetened them by handing him the portrait of Sir Christopher Wren that adds distinction and dignity to the £50 note.

'Quick,' I said. 'I want the names of the wines, in the order they've been set up there.' I winked. 'A little joke, you understand.'

'Yes, sir. I understand.'

He took a stub of pencil from an apron pocket and scribbled a list of the wines that were to be tasted.

'The first one's the one at this end of the row, and so on,' he said. He smiled and added, 'I hope you enjoy your little joke, sir.'

I rejoined our host as he was falling about, so to speak, laughing at one of Vincent's cunning anecdotes. Then the other guests started to arrive.

Dr Adzug made Crocodile Dundee look like a boy scout. Dr Adzug had the skin of a crocodile, tanned and crevassed by half a century's hot summers in the vineyards and on the race-courses of Australia. His fair hair was sun-bleached almost white. His eyes were pale blue, the whites yellowish with fine capillary threads of red. He opened his mouth wide when he smiled: his teeth were perfect.

While everyone was being introduced to everyone else, I had an opportunity to tell Vincent what I had obtained from the cellarman, and why.

'Of the eight Rieslings,' I said, 'Dr Adzug's is the fifth from the left.'

After one of those fulsome speeches of greeting which mean hardly anything except that the speaker is pleased to find he has an audience, the tasting began.

'D'you like Riesling?' Dr Adzug asked Vincent. Vincent has the appearance that makes strangers feel that his opinion is valuable.

'Yes, Dr Adzug, very much indeed. As a matter of fact, it happens to be the wine for which I have the highest esteem.'

'That's good to hear,' Dr Adzug said. 'But Steve's the name.'

'But when it comes to Riesling,' Vincent blandly continued, 'Catling here is your man. I don't think I've ever met anyone who knows Riesling – who loves Riesling – as he does. I await his verdict on the wines we are about to taste. His judgment shall be my guide.'

'Is that so? Well, Pat. Get tasting, boy!'

I frowned mildly, as if deprecating frivolity at a moment of such ... momentousness. I said:

'It's funny, I suppose; silly, really, perhaps; but I take wine rather seriously. I experience a sort of stage fright on an occasion such as this. The thing is, Dr Adzug – Steve – I *care*.'

Most people at wine tastings seem to take wine and themselves even more seriously than I, at first, pretended to. You know the dedicated wine-taster's pretentious ritual: holding the glass up to the light and looking at the colour as closely as a jeweller appraises a diamond; lowering the end of the nose into the glass and snuffling like a pig in search of truffles; pursing the lips like a judge about to pronounce or not pronounce a life sentence; taking a largish sip and running the wine around the teeth with the tip of the tongue; curling the tongue and trilling the wine against the palate and tonsils – and spitting the wine into a sort of cuspidor. Doing everything with the wine but drinking it!

My technique is simpler. All I do is slosh the wine back.

'You don't fool around,' the Australian observed. I couldn't be sure whether he was sympathetic or critical. After all, he had travelled halfway around the world to promote his wine. Possibly he was more orthodox than his orange tweed suit and brown and white Tattersall waistcoat suggested.

'I see you don't spit it out,' he said.

'No, never. I don't hold with that spitting-it-out routine.'

'Once wine gets into Catling's mouth it's a goner,' Vincent confirmed.

'I swallow it,' I said. 'I don't like to see alcohol wasted.'

There was no doubt that I had made Dr Adzug notice me.

It was time for the next phase: the talk. I quite enjoy all the competitive wine talk, the metaphors which wine men coin in vain attempts to describe what different wines taste like. Describing wine is even more difficult than describing the sound of music. So now the guests tried to outdo each other. In this exercise as well my method was conspicuously simple.

'This Riesling,' one little prig said, indicating Bottle Number Four, 'is broken slates on a terraced house on a rainy day in Newcastle.'

'Number Seven is the prettiest,' insisted another wine genius whose muse was probably sulking after too many tastings and not enough swallowings. 'This wine has the not-quite-dry, cool scent of an apple-orchard on a midsummer evening when the dew is beginning to form on the flowers in the long grass.'

'Bullshit!' I muttered, loud enough for Australian ears, and for an Australian grin.

'There is only one great Riesling here today,' I said. Dr Adzug stopped grinning. 'There are seven thin little Rieslings that would do no harm in a bowl of punch so long as you added plenty of rum. There are seven very ordinary, rather acid Rieslings. There is one of which I plan to drink a lot more. It is an elixir fit for heroes.'

My arrogant, dogmatic manner first silenced the other guests and then provoked some indignant whispering. One elder states-man of the wine-tasting circuit wanted to know who I thought I was.

'All right!' Vincent said, as if challenging me. 'Which is it?'

'There is no doubt,' I said. '*The* wine is from Bottle Number Five. It's obviously a Riesling from the Barossa Valley. What do you think, Vincent?'

'In my opinion, it's nectar for the gods. I'm going to stick my neck out at this point,' Vincent said with a sort of aw-shucks good-natured smile, against himself if he turned out to be mistaken. 'I think it's a 1989 Schloss Adzug. Well, Steve?'

Stefan Adzug nodded vigorously and led the burst of applause.

As he, Vincent and I enjoyed another bottle of the pleasant, well-chilled Barossa wine, Steve said:

'I wonder if you can imagine what a kick this has given me. In the past ten years, I've heard a hell of a lot of condescending guff about my wine from you pommy – from you English wine experts. You're a couple of beauts. I'll tell you what I'd like you to do.'

This was the moment that I'd been looking forward to.

'I'd like you to be my guests for lunch.'

I was not overwhelmed.

'At the Henry Ayers Restaurant.'

I must have looked blank. Vincent certainly did. Steve grinned more widely than ever.

'It's one of the better restaurants in Adelaide,' he said.

22

S TEVE had a few more days' business to finish in London.
   'Don't pack a lot,' he told Vincent and me. 'We'll get to Oz
in time for the last days of summer. It'll be informal where we're
going. If you need anything I'll get it for you when we get there.'

He took us by Qantas (which has an unblemished safety
record), first class, straight to Adelaide, with only two brief
fuelling stops. One day we were shivering in cold drizzle;
twenty-six hours later we were in sunshine under the immense
blue Australian sky.

Lunch at the Ayers House was very good. In the words of the
proprietor, 'this is more than one of the stately homes of
Australia; it is part of South Australian history. The first part was
built for William Paxton in 1846, just ten years after settlement
of the colony. In 1858 Paxton sold it to Henry Ayers, later
knighted and a Premier of South Australia.'

'I'm sure they're fascinated,' Steve said. 'But we're all kind of
tired, and we only had six dinners on the way over. Let's have
some menus – and the wine list.'

I liked the oysters, from Sydney. They were not too large, but
plump and creamy.

'We have a good Chablis to go with them,' Steve said. He was
right about that. He was right about all the wines of that long,
long lunch.

'Get a proper night's sleep,' he said. 'If this were an odd-
numbered year, we'd be back in The Valley in time for the
Barossa Valley Vintage Festival. It's a two-day Mardi Gras. You
could have competed in the grape-treading. You'll have to come
back next year. In the meantime, we'll do our best to entertain
you with a festival of our own at the Schloss.'

'I have a feeling we're going to get schlossed,' Vincent said.
He was *very* tired.

176

After showing us his own vineyards, his highly mechanised winery, and the castle, Steve escorted us on a wine-tasting tour of the rest of the Barossa district.

'Here's a good omen,' Vincent said, showing me the map. 'The Valley is situated between Mount Lofty and St Vincent's Gulf.'

'Vincent's influence follows us everywhere,' I agreed.

It followed us even when Steve took us in his private plane to Alice Springs and Ayers Rock.

'The Rock's named after that restaurant,' Vincent pointed out. Australian hospitality was softening his brain. And mine.

Steve told us about the man who built the first hotel in Alice Springs, himself, by hand, with the help of only one Aboriginal boy.

'I wish you had been able to meet Lycurgus,' Steve said. 'Lycurgus J. R. Underdown invented roof cricket. They used to play it on the roof of his hotel. He was known as the Mad Wicketkeeper.'

We spent one very lively morning drinking ice-cold lagers in The Bull Bar, a back room in the Stuart Arms Hotel.

'Lycurgus was a pioneer of pioneers,' Steve said, raising his glass in an umpteenth toast. 'You've got to have the pioneer spirit even now to live in The Alice. They have swimming pools now and barbies on irrigated lawns behind suburban bungalows, but you still have to be a pioneer! Here's to pioneers!'

He drank further toasts to kangaroos, emus, koalas and camels.

An opal miner on holiday from Coober Pedy, South Australia, where everyone lives below ground because the overground temperature reaches 140 degrees Fahrenheit, kept sending us rounds of drinks, and we kept retaliating.

There was a large poster, unusual in a barroom, warning that BOOZERS ARE LOSERS.

I seem to remember that we laughed like kookaburras up a gum tree.

23

IN retreat from the bright lights of the Australian Outback, I flew back to London and on to Cork.

When dazed by the culture shock of our globally homogenised civilisation, there is nothing so therapeutic as a week or two of plain food and plain theology. I was fed up to here with sauces and philsophical gimmicks which turn out to be no more than advertisements for themselves.

I applied for admission to Mount Melleray Abbey, in County Waterford. A Cistercian foundation established in 1833, Mount Melleray, like other monasteries, is always open to everyone who knocks on its doors. It welcomes Catholics and those of any other faith or no faith at all.

The Abbey is situated on six hundred acres of what was once called 'scrahan' or 'coarse land', on a rocky hillside on the southern slopes of the Knockmealdown Mountains. During the past 157 years, the monks, almost a hundred of them at any time, have cleared the land for farming and have planted many trees. The abbey itself, though its name shares the derivation of *mellifluous, honey-flowing*, is an austerely imposing edifice of dark grey granite. Arriving there, one feels sure that one is leaving the world of sitcoms and canned laughter.

The Guestmaster, Father Francis, accepted me with quietly efficient hospitality, without any comments on the weather or questions about the condition of my soul.

The Cistercians are an enclosed order. Visitors are housed in isolation. They have left the world (temporarily), but they cannot enter the heart of the Abbey. However, they are allowed into a hagioscopic gallery at the back of the church for as many, or as few, of the offices as they may want, at four-hour intervals day and night.

At Patrick Leigh Fermor observed, 'when thrown by chance

180

in touch with monasticism, [one] can glean from it much of the healing and mysterious enchantment for which, among other purposes, monasteries were built.'

Up one floor, my room was small, white and bare, with a bed, a desk and a chair, and a window overlooking a garden. A short distance along a narrow, grey corridor, there was a shower. Water was abundant, some of it sometimes hot. A lay brother, whose pale face, short beard and thick, steel-rimmed glasses reminded me of James Joyce, served three meals a day – breakfast, lunch and high tea – in a dining room on the ground floor.

The brother who worked in the kitchen and waited on the guests had lived in the Abbey for thirteen years, since he was twenty-two. He was friendly and liked to talk. When he was handing me poached eggs, baked beans, bread and butter and jam at teatime, he told me about a monk who used to grow his own tobacco and make 'very good cigars'.

At first, I was the only guest. The next day, however, two others arrived.

An English priest and I shared a table for lunch. He immediately confided that he was spending some time at Melleray to recover from a nervous breakdown.

'My parish is in Liverpool,' he said. 'We're supported largely by bingo and one-armed bandits in the church club. But last year the club lost twelve thousand pounds and I didn't know what to do. Our burglar alarm is very loud. When I turn it off, the police get upset. When it rings, it disturbs the neighbours. It's all very difficult.'

The second newcomer was a bearded American anthropologist in his twenties, from Seattle, Washington. He was dressed as if for mountaineering, with enormous, cleated boots and thick-ribbed high socks. He joined us for tea and proved to have logorrhoea.

'I come from an affluent background,' he said. The priest looked as if he was going to groan. 'It's difficult for me to relate objectively to the concept that the Chinese are God's people, even though I accept that they are.'

I went for a walk at sunset. The young American followed and caught up. The evening was cold and clear. As the pink faded and the blue darkened, Venus appeared.

'I was talking with Father Francis,' my companion said. 'I said if a dog loves its master it must have a soul. That love has to go somewhere when the dog dies, like your mother's and father's love.'

'What did Father Francis say?' I asked.

'Nothing much really.'

The American said he had met a group of 'very tall men' in Dublin. 'They tried to convert me to Korean mysticism, but I wasn't having any.'

As far as the guests are concerned, this community definitely is not a silent order.

The English priest was two bedrooms away. His snores made my window rattle.

The next day was grey, misty and wet. There was a soft susurrus through the conifers. It was a good day for thinking.

There were eggs, toast and tea for breakfast. Although there were several empty tables, the priest and the anthropologist came and sat with me.

'You know,' the American said, 'I think I could just move right into this monastery and settle down.'

The priest's response was waspish.

'They're fussy about whom they take.'

After an awkward silence, the American tried again.

'I think I have had a vision,' he said.

'Probably something you ate for supper,' commented the priest.

At the end of breakfast, the American lit a cigarette and announced: 'I'm going to take off. I've decided to go to Ethiopia to write a book about agricultural communities and God, from an anthropological point of view.'

When the young man left the table, the priest said he had not slept much.

'You aren't planning to use the toilet now, are you?' he asked anxiously.

I gave him a consoling quotation from St Augustine, whose works I was borrowing from the Abbey's excellent library:

'Join thyself to eternity and thou shalt find rest.'

The priest looked unconvinced and left the room mumbling.

I suppose most people's favourite Augustinian prayer is the one in which he asked God to give him chastity – 'but not yet.'

After tea, the monks and the guests were allowed to mingle in a small auditorium for a lecture on ecology and conservation by Dr Maire Mulcahy, of the Department of Zoology of University College, Cork. She looked like a slender Elizabeth Taylor in a pink tweed suit.

She discussed the biosphere, food chains, the balance between plant and animal life, pollution caused by burning fossil fuels, the world population explosion and food resources et cetera.

In the question period, there were only two questions:

1. 'If the money now spent on arms were spent on producing and distributing more food, would the world be well fed by the year 2,000?' and

2. 'Are you against the right of a flea to its place in the food chain?'

After breakfast the next day, one of the brothers recalled a debate he once had with a visiting atheist.

'He said there was a parasite that burrows into its host's neck to lay eggs, so that the offspring will be able to eat the dead host. "How could a benign creator arrange such a system?" the atheist asked. I answered: "How do you know the host doesn't like it?" '

That story made me feel better about some of the hosts I have burrowed into.

I found J. B. Morton's book about his friend Hilaire Belloc, and enjoyed the last lines of a Belloc song:

> *What did Eve say to Adam,*
> *The saucy little madam?*
> *Oh, Adam, you should eat more fruit.*

After nearly two weeks of long walks and reading and long nights' sleep, I suddenly felt regenerated. It was time to go back into the world.

I had not thought recently about freeloading. I asked Father Francis for my bill. He said the words I have so often loved to hear:

'There is no charge.'

Ahakista, West Cork

A NOTE ON THE AUTHOR

Patrick Skene Catling has published many works of fiction and humour, including, appropriately enough, his first book, *Better Than Working*. Patrick Skene Catling lives in Ireland.